Paul Ferrini reconnects us to the Spirit Within,
to that place where even our deepest wounds can be healed.

JOAN BORYSENKO

Paul Ferrini's wonderful books show us a way to walk lightly
with joy on planet Earth.

GERALD JAMPOLSKY

Paul Ferrini's work is a must read for all people who are ready
to take responsibility for their own healing.

JOHN BRADSHAW

Paul Ferrini's books are the most important I have read.
I study them like a Bible.

ELISABETH KÜBLER-ROSS

Paul Ferrini's writing will inspire you to greater insights
and understandings, to more clarity and a grander resolve
to make changes in your life that can truly change the world.

NEALE DONALD WALSCH

Paul Ferrini is an important teacher in the new millenium.
Reading his work has been a major awakening for me.

IYANLA VANZANT

Paul Ferrini is a modern day Kahlil Gibran— poet, mystic,
visonary, teller of truth.

LARRY DOSSEY

I feel that this work comes from a continuous friendship with
the deepest Part of the Self. I trust its wisdom.

COLEMAN BARKS

Book Design by Lisa Carta
Cover Art: The Kiss, by Gustav Klimt

Library of Congress Card Number 2009912491
ISBN # 978-1-879159-81-5

Manufactured in the United States of America

# When Love
# Comes as a Gift

*Meeting the Soul Mate in this Life*

# PAUL FERRINI

# Table of Contents

## PART TWO

## PART THREE

## PART FOUR

## PART FIVE

## PART SIX

## PART SEVEN

# Preface

$\mathcal{E}$ach partner who comes to dance with us teaches us something and brings us the gift of connection in new ways. Through each, we touch what is possible for us to create with another. In this sense, the soul mate is not just one person, but a work in progress, a tapestry being woven out of light and shadow, hope and fear.

Each partner who comes to dance with us teaches us something and brings us the gift of connection in new ways. Through each, we touch what is possible for us to create with another. In this sense, the soul mate is not just one person, but a work in progress, a tapestry being woven out of light and shadow, hope and fear.

Every lover we have prepares us to meet the Beloved. Each one brings a lesson and a gift. And each defers to another who brings a deeper gift and a more compelling lesson.

As we learn to honor ourselves, we attract partners who challenge us to become more conscious about the choices that we make. Gradually, we open our hearts to the potential of creating intimacy on all levels.

This full-chakra embrace opens to us when we have substantially completed our inner work. And then it is no longer a temporal affair. It is Spirit come to flesh. It is the indwelling Presence of Love, blessing us and lifting us up.

It is both a gift and a responsibility, both a promise made and a promise fulfilled.

# Part One

# The Storm

Rain comes into the heart and into the earth as an awakening presence. The lake behind the house is pummeled by billions of droplets as the sky descends in one cascading black cloud after another, and wind drives the stirred waters of the lake from one edge to the other.

Your hands on my body have the same effect. I am like the palm caught up in the cyclone, the wind spinning around it, threatening to uproot it, driving it right to the edge of extinction.

No man or woman in her right mind would have asked to be penetrated in this way. The wind and the rain hold every thing hostage. Even the ducks on the pond are gathered into the spinning world, rising up to feel the wind as they beat their wings and settle back into the turgid waters.

You don't have to be a winged beast to be invaded. All living things are penetrated by the storm and are pregnant with its energy. You and I are just wombs waiting to be filled with falling leaves, twigs and bark chips, as the trees shake all around us.

Last night on the beach, we were just as hungry for each other, rolling around like two ravenous puppies in the sand. Yet there is something completely impersonal in this. The storm comes and goes in our hearts and in our hands, grabbing any body part it can reach, and then releasing it, as the surf breaks on the beach and pulls back in the undertow.

Without nature, there would be no way to understand the push and the pull or the sweep of eye or hand across these beaches and meadows of our hearts. Every cell in the body is alive and moving in some spontaneous mudra or dance and we are two warriors on the beach wielding the wands of blue light under the spinning black clouds and silver sands.

Birds fly out from the heart and sleep under our feet. We are part of the stirred world, the ecstatic minions beyond ordinary sight. Our kisses are not kisses, but armies invading in the night, populating the earth, and disappearing at first light.

You are not a woman nor I a man, but we are some other thing that uses our arms and legs and torsos to do its provocative dance, commanding the rain and wind to come to the beach. I used to think soul mates did another type of dance. But I was completely wrong.

This dance is beyond you or me. It takes place in our bloodstream and drives its energy up through our bones. It has nothing per se to do with your body or mine. We are just temporary hosts.

The energy did not ask for permission to embody within us. And it does not ask for our permission to leave.

We have no say, nor can we protest the violation of our

boundaries. When the wind comes, there is no flesh that does not become wind, and when the waters rise there is no hand or arm that does not move like a fin through the raging waters.

No one prepared us for this.

At the wedding of wind and waves, the stars shake in the heavens and hearts are shattered in some arcane ritual only our bodies can understand. The body is just a scarf that blows in the wind and eventually comes free, leaving us naked, like Noah after the first storm came, shaking the earth with thunder in the sky and explosions of light all over the rushing waters.

In the ecstatic world, the body is the price you pay. It is swept up and sent spinning on a single leg, rooted in some hidden center of the storm, driven like a sail in a circular wind, round and around, with arms and legs trembling.

Rumi knew of this, but he did not tell us. Had we known that we would be molested, violated, penetrated by a force greater than any we had known, it is not likely we have chosen to come to this beach. Had I known, even the power of your eyes would not have been enough to draw me here. I would have held back. I would have left the beach to the wind and the rain and the black rumbling clouds.

When the energy of earth meets the energy of sky, the mirror on the lake's surface ceases to be empty. It is filled by angry gods, bobbing and weaving in some strange ceremonial dance.

Beware all of you who are calling out for your soul mates. The soul mate is not the soft one you expect. He is Shiva and she is Shakti, the embodiment of the storm.

You will not live through the night when the soul mate comes. Something you have held onto for lifetimes will be ripped away from you.

And the gods will dance on your torn body. For they know, you have finally been humbled and vanquished.

# The Fire of the Gods

Today I am ablaze
like a fire driven by winds,
leaping from tree to tree,
ravaging the mountaintop.

The fire cannot be contained.
It burns as long as the wind blows.
If you come too close,
you too will be set ablaze.

Are you sure you are ready to burn
for the rest of your life?

I do not seem to have a choice.

As soon as the lightning strikes
the nearby timbers are lit
and a wind as if from another life
rises to meet me.

People stop and ask "Are you all right?
Is everything okay with you?"
And what can I say?
How does one carry on as usual?

When our eyes meet, our tears flow,
spilling into the flames,
yet the fire burns on,
hissing like a snake about to strike.

I know the gods are laughing,
as my heart does its epileptic dance,
shaking, convulsing, till I am forced
to fall to the ground.

They take a strange pleasure
in my loss of decorum and control.
"We finally have you
where we want you," they tell me.

Like Prometheus,
I learn to burn without being consumed,
to leap through the air
without moving.

Is this the reward or the price
of knowledge? Perhaps it is both.
Now you too must pay the price.

Zeus has sent his dagger of light
into the base of your spine,
igniting the driftwood
hurled high on the beach.

Now I am not the only one who burns.

We must suffer the divine will
if we would become one with it.

It is painful, yet ecstatic.
And there is no escape from this embrace.
We are entwined together
like the branches on the tree of life.

In the salt air, the snake-tongued flames
lick every twisted sinew of our bodies
until we lose consciousness.

Hanging onto life now only by a thread
we dimly hear the roar of the flames
knowing we are too far away
to be saved by the sea.

# *Peace*

After the storm subsides, grey sky yields to highlights of white and blue. Earth is refreshed and invigorated. You can smell the aroma the stormed awakened.

The lake is placid, as if it were a different body of water: serene and still, mirroring everything around it in its stark grey-black beauty.

As strong and impulsive as the storm was, its aftermath is peaceful and steady. The simple rhythms of nature reassert themselves. The heart at the center of the earth beats steadily and the heart in the center of our bodies sounds its gentle diastole as our breath slows and becomes regular.

I return to the world, looking quietly into your eyes, or holding your hand and walking beside you. It is simple and easy. I know that I am in my right place.

When you first approached me, I recognized you and knew what you were going to say:

"You are my brother, my friend, my husband. Your voice is the voice I have always heard in the secret chambers of my heart. I know its resonance. You have not touched me with your hands, yet I know how your fingers will feel as they run through my hair or caress my thighs. I have never kissed you, yet I know the feel of your lips on mine. When I look into your eyes, currents of fire shoot through every cell of my body. I know you. I recognize you. Do you remember me? Do you know me in the way that I know you?"

And you knew how I would respond: "Yes, I remember

you. In your smile, all the love I have ever known rises to meet me. In the sound of your voice, I hear the intonations of generations of women I have called mother, or daughter, or wife. Yes, I know you. Yet I can hardly believe my eyes or my ears. I can hardly believe we are standing face to face."

In the mirror of the lake, we stand eye to eye, soul to soul. Although we just met, we are not strangers. Everything that others would take years to find out about you or about me, we already know. There is total transparency here, for no secrets are possible between us.

As we walk and my hand rests on your hip, it knows that it has always been there and your hip knows it too. We do not touch each other as lovers who are discovering each other do. My body already knows yours. My soul already knows your soul. We drift into each other like two energies merging. There are no boundaries. I feel what you feel.

Without this energy moving us spontaneously in and out of each other our behavior might be suspect. We could be accused of unhealthy bonding, fusing or codependence. But with the energy there is nothing inappropriate or unhealthy. When I touch you, it is not me touching you. There is no me and you. There is just touching. The one who touches and the one being touched are the same.

Everyone wants this. People go to workshops and read books on soul mates hoping to learn how to create this in their lives. But they are all wasting their time and their money.

This cannot be created. This is a gift.

The gift came. It did not come the way we expected it to come or at the time we expected it. It came on its own terms, according to its own timetable. It knocked and we opened.

That was it.

You cannot say no to an open door when your beloved is on the other side of the threshold. You cannot *not* go through the door. The idea that you can say no to that person or that you can reject the gift when it is offered to you is completely absurd. Even the greatest sadist cannot do this.

You might be able to reject or push away a lesser love, but you cannot reject or push away a love like this. It envelops you and occupies you. You cannot stand apart from it.

Our bodies are like super charged magnets. The polarities are already in place. As soon as we open our hearts, the attraction is so intense, so powerful, nothing can keep us apart.

# *Tethered to the Tides*

The search for the matching shells
was for naught.
Each shard left behind by wind and waves
was unique, confirming
the solitary journey.

Yet a tiny hope did survive
that somewhere invisible to the eye,
there would live another shell
of similar shape and hue,
shining in the breaking surf.

On the surface, we knew
that ours would be an imperfect union
and that to find what we seek
we would have to go deep and suffer
the push and pull of the tides.

Real love forces us to dive
beneath the surface,
where the shells toss and turn,
thrown onto the beach only to be
pulled back by the ebbing tide.

In that crucible, we are deafened
by the thunder of the waves
and blinded by the crystalline light
that shines above the waves
as they shatter on the sand.

That is where the alchemy happens,
turning fear in on itself,
carving out a space of surrender.
That is where trust is born
and love can enter.

It is from that cavernous place
That I heard you call out to me,
and felt the despair
of not knowing how to reach you.
But all that is over now.

The sparkle in your eyes, the tears
of gratitude, speak volumes
of the inner work that has been done
to bring forth this synergy,
this joining of two into one.

Enough said.

From this place only hearts can speak
and they are mute.
Our story is written by the tides
and buried in the sand
beyond the reach of shallow seekers.

One day another hand will reach in
and pluck this shell from the surf
and then our story will be known.
But for now, it is a mystery
only we can know.

Let others come and knock on this door.
It will not open.
The mystery of love reveals itself
only to the Lover, only to those
who have risked everything.

No one else could possibly understand.

# Qumrum

You were told that you were being imprinted with me, cell by cell. Now we know that those were not just words, but revelation.

With our cells vibrating in resonance, an energy field is generated around us. A vortex surrounds and envelops us. When we step even an inch beyond it in mind or heart, we can feel the tearing of the energy skin, and a pull back into the safety of the center. In this energy body, there is a shared heart beating, a resonating chord absorbing the sound of singular notes into their harmonic.

This is the energy body of incarnate love. It is the same body, the same womb that gave birth to the divine homunculus we know as Jesus, born of two spiritual equals in their time of flowering.

The virgin birth was not from Mary's womb, but from the energy body of Joseph and Mary, vibrating with the Holy Spirit. They brought life unto life and light unto light. The greatest planetary teacher of the spiritual law of equality was born of two equals, male and female, in their prime of life. Jesus was the fruit of that womb.

The womb is a temple in the spinning world, a place of ingathering and imprinting. It is the inner sanctuary, the incubation chamber, the heart inside the reach of the hands.

The womb seals in, guards and protects the developing fetus from the demands and fetters of the world. After birth, another protective covering descends to provide emotional support and security for the child. In time, the womb becomes a schoolroom filled by loving teachers. They receive the young Jesus and bless him. His parents have prepared him well. He is properly balanced and aligned, a perfect harmony of male and female energies. He is given to his teachers now.

At age seven, he enters the secret mystery school deep in the caves at Qumrum. There he is taught the power of prayer and opens to receive the Divine energy. In this temple hidden from sight, the timeless teaching is revealed to him and he is prepared for his spiritual journey. By the age of fourteen, Jesus already knows his destiny.

Out of the womb into the waiting arms of the world comes the fruit of Mary and Joseph, the shining light of their lights, the young master on fire with the truth.

# *Synergy*

The energy of love is not born of one, but of two becoming one. It is a magnetic force that erases boundaries, allowing the essence of both to interpenetrate and commingle.

From the union of true lovers, new creatures are born and the lovers themselves are transformed. The synergy of lovers engenders all of the mystical beasts of mythology: The Unicorn (union of hoof and wing, earth and sky), the Satyr (union of man and bull, reason and sexuality), and the Mermaid (union of woman and fish, sensation and feeling). These creatures symbolize real states of psychological integration.

The union of soul mates is neither homogenous nor contained. It is volatile, hungry, explosive. It expresses strong male and strong female energy in a kind of alternating current. It is completely energetic and polarized.

Without each other, the lovers cannot express both polarities simultaneously in time and space. But with each other, they do it effortlessly, rhythmically, and ecstatically. Everyone who comes near them feels their energy and is transformed by it.

They come to each other out of a deep and boundless yearning that cannot be put into words. It is the force and trajectory of their essence. But to find each other, each must refine and mature. Each must become empowered and whole. Each must surrender the blocks to love within his or her heart. And only then is their meeting possible.

When the time of joining comes, the final block is released. And then they are changed forever.

# *Morning Kiss*

*What is the price of a kiss? Your life!*   Rumi

Under the cover of sleep
the body lies awake,
gathering itself
between the clouds
and the whale sounds
at 4:00 AM.

I feel you next to me,
yet miles away
where the sun plummets
beneath the horizon,
lost in some sea
of remembered tears.

You hide your pain well
but at night
the veils open
and the ghosts come out
to dance on the waters
where the ship went down.

No, you did not deserve
that wreck on the shoals,
where you disappeared
with the ship, your oars
set adrift, your children
scattered in the wind.

Yet I remember you
as you once were, walking proudly
through the streets of an ancient city,
your white linen garments
lifted by the gentle
Mediterranean breezes,

your smile riveting the eyes
of all who behold you.
No, you do not deserve
this night haunted
by strange voices
and unsettling dreams.

Gently, I place my hand
on your back
as you turn over, the hand
that has never stopped touching you
throughout all the nights
we have remained apart.

Do not be afraid.
I have the tiller now.
It does not matter how
the heavens spin around us;
we will weather the storm
and return to the harbor.

As I listen to you breathe
I hear voices chanting
and see the dancing of bodies
around the ceremonial fire.
Our love was consecrated
in a time long before this one.

We were given to each other then,
but had lessons to learn
with others. Time and space
came between us,
and the shell that enclosed us
was pulled asunder.

Now the ragged edges
have been smoothed and polished
by the shifting tides.
They do not quite fit together
as before. Each half
has learned to dance alone.

Yet there is the memory
of how and where the joining was,
the seamless fit of arms and legs,
eyes and lips,
the memory of
an indivisible wholeness.

Dawn comes today
caressed by clouds,
propelled by a soft, grey wind,
and you arise to begin your day
as you would have begun
any other.

Only today it is not the same.
Today is pregnant
with voices from the past
never heard before,
angelic sounds of children singing
at the edge of night.

Today, the promise given
has been received
and here, in the soft grey light
hearts open, lips parted,
is the kiss we have been waiting for
all our lives.

# The Call of the Heart

The eyes are the light of the soul and there are oceanic depths there. Every day we go deeper into those depths. The fear of annihilation is powerless to stop us. We understand that it is our destiny to die into each other.

Like water, you are infinitely strong. In your fury, you could rip apart my hull and shatter my sails, but you prefer to caress me and support me.

Something quintessential has shifted in each of us now. Without the protection of the ego, we are defenseless and naked. There is nothing in each other that we can avoid or look away from.

You are my changing mirror. It cannot be argued or disputed.

# *Shimmering*

Today the cool summer breeze reigns
as it did in my childhood
digging for fish in the sparkling waters of the river
or playing hide and seek in the cornfields,

investigating every hidden cave
or oblique angle of hill
and singing out like some off-key buoy
or ghostly didgeridoo.

Today, sails billow and stretch,
the branches in full leaf bow and sway,
and the skirts of the women dancers
lift slightly as they turn and spin.

Today, light and movement
invade every dark and obstinate thing
and even the dullest surfaces
shimmer in the breeze.

Today, no flower or blade of grass,
no arm or wing can resist
the persistent, resurrecting
power of the wind.

This is a day we will remember
for many years, a day when life
is so sharp and pungent,
no neurotic or self pitying thought

can stand the bright, effervescent light
or get stuck in the shadows
of the windswept clouds
as they pass by overhead.

Today, death comes and goes
without leaving a trace.
Nothing stagnates
or grinds to a halt.

Nothing rots or festers,
covers or clings. Everything moves
with quickness and grace,
and life reigns in its fullness.

# Resistance

Sometimes the energy that rises is so intense it seems that I am going to lose consciousness. It is disconcerting and destabilizing. I don't know how to shift myself to contain it.

It wants something from me I have not learned to give. It requires some sacrifice I have not been willing to make.

When I try to back away and step down the connection between us, a black hopelessness comes in, and I realize I cannot go there. I cannot turn away. The old defense mechanisms don't work. They don't even apply.

As long as I continue to believe that you are you and I am I, I can go though the motions of separation, but then they sputter and crash into the blackness. I know that schism is an illusion, an old one that can no longer be believed or tolerated.

When this truth is accepted, the energy comes back full force. It rises like a wave from the bowels of the earth and moves up through the solar plexus and the heart. It wants to push all the way up through the throat and third eye and be released through the crown chakra.

I would like to stop touching you, stop pouring gasoline on a fire that is already raging. But stopping is not possible. All of the mind's schemes to dampen the flames are useless and irrelevant. The hands cannot stop touching any more than the heart can stop beating. As long as there is breath in the body, the flames will burn.

Yes, this is a form of suffering, but I must keep remembering that Christ will take all. The body, the heart, and the mind are being purified in the Spiritual Fire. Any untruth, any resistance, any fear, doubt or disharmony will be consigned to the flames and destroyed.

# The Visitation

She is not an ordinary human being.

Although she appears in a woman's body,
her beauty surpasses the beauty
of that graceful body
infusing it with light and tenderness.

Looking into her sparkling blue eyes
I try to confess my feelings to her,
but the words are stolen from my lips
before I can speak them.

Although my hands are on fire
I cannot caress her hair or her face.
The closer I come, the more
her body fades away.

Its seems our embrace took place
before these bodies existed
and will persist beyond the veil
when it is torn asunder.

Beware all you lovers.
Although you yearn for this,
you do not understand
that it will change you forever.

# Trysts

The beach has become your bridal bed. The wind itself is a tongue hiding somewhere in moonlight where the sands shift to accommodate your weight.

Now the bee goes to his favorite flower. While he eats, he gets drunk on the ambrosia and stumbles out of the inner sanctum inebriated and shaky, forgetting that he has wings to fly.

The transformation of the profane has already begun. The dancing bodies have softened in the flames, inviting all the shamans in. Now, we climb the hidden steps of Jacob's ladder and sail into the dark skies to destinations beyond space and time.

My hands move on your buttocks and up the curve of your back drawing you into a full body embrace. You are the fireworks, but I am the dark womb of sky that embraces you, the strong arms into which your body falls when it is completely released.

The Shekinah* descends from the heavens, riding on waves of sound and light as it moves mysteriously through the three-dimensional world. And we do not know it has been here until we open our eyes and begin to brush off the moonlight and the sand.

---

*heavenly chariot

# Meeting the Beloved

The young man came to me in my dreams and asked: "How can I meet my beloved?"

"You must yearn for it with all your heart," I told him. "You must place this desire for the Beloved above all other desires and be patient with it. It must ripen and you must become strong and confident. The Beloved cannot come to one who is not patient or who has not learned to deeply know and love himself.

"The Beloved is the gift one receives when one has learned to love oneself without conditions. Love and honor yourself," I told him, "and before long you will hear her footsteps approaching.

"Nothing else can prepare you for the moment when S/he rises to meet you. You will be propelled into a different world. Your arms and legs will move with a passion you did not know that you possessed. Like a crazed bee you will dive headfirst into the flower not caring if you ever come out.

"But that is just the beginning. Falling in love is but an initiation to a greater vocation. Love comes as a gift, but the quality of the gift can only be realized when it is understood and put to work. Those who enter the flower, must learn to make honey in the heart.

Once that happens, there will be no falling out of love, no crash after each epiphany, but highs and lows will ride together through the ebb and flow of life."

He thanked me and went back into the world of dreams.

I do not know where he came from or where he went. I know only that such a person will not fail.

A dream that guides our waking life is not just a dream. It is a compass. It keeps us on course through all the twists and turns. It brings us face to face...We are witnesses to that.

## On the Boardwalk

The mangroves twist and turn along the boardwalk that skirts the little cove off the Intercoastal Waterway where small boats can pull in and tie up. Protected from sight by the dense and twisted limbs and their greenery, the boardwalk wraps around the inlet on its way to the beach.

As you turn to face the water, I wrap you in my arms and begin caressing you from behind. I feel your body sink into mine and move in a gentle rhythm as my hands explore your breasts, your belly and your thighs. For a few moments, we become like mangrove limbs intricately twisted together and inseparable.

I admire your complete surrender. You trust me with your heart and with your body, moving like a dancer beyond the climax of the dance into a blissful and contented peace. I feel it in your body. I see it in your flushed face and in the poetry of your eyes.

Now I begin to see the truth of all this: to have everything, you must give yourself completely. By trusting, we descend more deeply into the place where boundaries disappear and Lover and Beloved are one and the same.

For a few moments we rest in complete silence and then the human world intervenes. A small noisy boat rounds the bend, belching smoke and gasoline fumes. It comes straight for us and then stops and turns the other way.

But the violation has already occurred. The fumes scratch at our throats and we are forced to withdraw from our mangrove haven.

Walking north along the beach, we leave the million dollar properties behind to get to the wild places, not stopping until we are surrounded by seawater and sand, palms and ocean pines.

The small birds walk with us, dancing in and out of the breaking waves, dipping their feathery butts in the frothy water and then shaking the water from their wings. For them bathing is like breathing. They do it constantly. It is part of the rhythm of their lives.

# Part Two

# Waking Dream

We are just ordinary people, yet love has set us its mark on us. Love has moved into our minds and set up housekeeping. Love has sent its armies into our hearts. Now they are occupied countries.

I have watched you looking down, pretending that you don't see me gazing at you. I have watched you knitting those multi-colored threads. I have seen the lump in your throat woven into the tapestry.

Your yearning for me is muted, subdued, yet I know that a fire rages in your heart. I have heard the sound of your heart crying out in the night. It has drawn me here.

At dawn, I wake up beside you and watch you sleep. I touch you softly and gradually feel your body responding. Your breath comes faster now as you begin to wake up. "Is this for real or is it just a dream?" you ask.

"It is both," I say. I am touching you all over, but I am not here. The place next to you in the bed is empty. The sheets have not even been wrinkled.

You feel like I am here, but I am not. I am in another place, dreaming of you."

# *Bliss*

Returning to the cold snowy heart of winter,
to the mountains anchored to earth
by bare branches

returning by the road twisting north
through the frozen fields
and the pine forests,

coming to meet you
from a different time and place,
a different life, now forgotten.

This morning the sun rises red and purple
at the horizon, suffusing the sky
from east to west

in gradations of roseate light.
In the black womb of space
the sun is a fiery ball consuming everything.

Here it is a flower opening, a gentle breath
like the one I hear as you turn
to nestle your head against my chest.

It is for this moment of surrender that I live,
not for the storm with all its passion
or the peaceful aftermath,

but for the gentle motion
of your trust in me and in us.
That is where the energy abides.

That is the place of its origin.
It is from there that love arises.
and it is there that it returns

when its work is done.
It is not a place of struggle or striving,
of action or result, but a place

of utter contentment,
a place of wholeness, a place of bliss
without beginning or end.

# The Fountain

We were together in the forest, exploring the streams, chasing each other along the pine needle footpaths. You were quick and unpredictable, like a wood nymph. I reached out for you and you danced away, laughing at my frustration. Whenever I thought I had lost you, our eyes met unexpectedly through the canopy of leaves and flowers.

Sometimes, at night, your eyes are like that. Looking deeply into those green pools of light, waves of love enter me and move through my body. Every cell is kissed from the inside out. All night, my blood throbs through the veins and arteries, like drums beating in the dark silence. I have no respite.

When the first rays of light rise above the mountains to the east, I hear the sound of rushing water. It comes up out of the ground like a geyser, forming a deep pool all around me. I let myself down into the black water. It is so hot it nearly takes my breath away.

I relax in the steamy water and fall back to sleep. When I wake up, you are running your fingers through my hair.

Around the mountain pool, there is new aroma, a scent of almond and cedar. We wonder where it has come from, not knowing that it comes from us.

We have become a rare wine. Beware those who sip from this cup!

# *Dancing in the Flames*

Before dawn, hundreds of ships set sail through the dark waters. While too far away to be seen, you can hear their engines rumbling in the distance.

Gradually, in the blackness, the ships soften and disappear, giving way to hundreds of red rose petals, torn and bleeding across the black sky.

As the crimson sun lifts itself out of the dark waters, gulls and dolphins play in the shimmering light.

The journey is ecstatic. It is all about energy and reflection. At one moment we are sitting still. In another, there is unspeakable movement.

At daybreak in Vermont, the maples are ablaze with orange light. At dawn in New Mexico, the aspens are shaking silvery in the wind.

Every day awakens us to our purpose. We are each called to travel through the night and rise like the Phoenix at the break of day. We are each called to our solar purpose: to shine, to burn, to light the way.

And some, like us, are called to burn together, every thought we have of each other feeding the flames like seasoned wood thrown into the fire. We burn, yet we are not consumed. Only the thoughts and feelings that run shy of love are licked away in the flames.

You see, the master sculptor has begun working on the stone. Slabs are falling away. The eyes, the hands, the lips are gradually revealing themselves.

Because we live now entwined around each other like wisteria vines in full bloom, others are drawn to us without knowing why. Lovers come to sit on the bench beneath our arbor. They whisper endearments they think no one has expressed before.

They do not know yet what we know.

To love is to die a thousand deaths. It is to be purified in the fire, to burn without being consumed. For the fire cannot put itself out. The eternal cannot become temporal. Our dance, once begun, can never end.

# The Ceremony

Others are married by clergy.

We are married by wind and rain.
We are take our vows
in the eye of the storm
while the wind blows
around us.

Others emerge with official papers.
We emerge with sap smeared
on our hands and feet
and only the trees
as our witnesses.

We asked the rabbi
to come and bless us,
but he wouldn't come,
nor would the priest
or the Sufi sheik.

They were afraid of God's wrath.
They were afraid
that the wind and the waves
would rise up
and smite them.

I do not blame them
for not coming.

Had I known the fury
your eyes would bring,
or the havoc
wrought by your hands
on my body

I would not have come either.
I would have stayed
in the square,
playing chess
with the rabbi.

I would have closed my eyes
and sat there
like a statue
when the hem of your dress
brushed my leg.

I would have refused to hear
your innocent voice
when you asked me
to walk with you
out into the meadow.

But it's too late now.
The act is done.
Life as my life
has come to an end.

Now every thought I think,
every emotion I feel,
every sensation
in my body
belongs to you.

# A New Continent

Somewhere in the middle of the sea, a new continent is growing. Mountains are rising up. New fauna and flora are taking refuge there. Children shelter under the green canopies and sit on the massive roots that reach down deeply into the earth. No one is denied the fruits of love or its shelter.

You see, the egg of time is cracking open. It is only a matter of time before the shell shatters and the dove of peace spreads his wings over us.

# Prayer

Mother
We have opened our hearts.
We have emptied our minds.

We have thrown the old skins out
and bought new skins
to receive the new wine.

We are ready now
to receive your infinite love.

# Surrendering

Before this dance had begun, you were already moving your hips to the sound of the drums. Now I follow your footsteps into the night.

Your lips are softer than they have ever been. And you pull me toward you in a new way, so deep and so familiar I wonder how either one of us ever lived without the other.

As we return home from the beach, I can feel that your arm rests differently on my shoulder. Now, you are not afraid to let all of your weight rest on me. You don't have to hold back anymore. You let yourself sink into me with total trust.

# *Cornucopia*

Until both of us trust, the real dance of love cannot begin. The rituals leading up to that moment are preliminary.

To find the shared heart, we have to peel off our separate skins, transcend our selfish wants and needs, and let go of our pictures of the way we think that things should be. To stay in that heart we must be courageous enough to be naked and vulnerable with each other.

We do not have to be perfect for each other. We just need to be willing to accept when it isn't easy, to stretch when we are contracted, to acknowledge our pain when we hurt, and to feel each other's pain even when we cannot fix it.

Our compassion for each other opens the door to an ancient place, a secret sanctuary. As we enter, we understand that this is not the first time we have been there. We know that it is time to complete the journey we began together a long time ago.

All the fruits that we have gathered in other times and places can be tasted now. For hours we have smelled the aroma of freshly baked bread in the oven. It is time now to bring the warm, crusty loaves out to the table, pull them open and let the butter melt over them. It is time to bring out the wine aged to perfection and pour it into the tall glasses.

The time we have prepared for has arrived. There is no more inner and outer, high and low, male and female, you or me. There is just essence co-mingled and a profound congruence between how we feel and what we say or do.

# *Readiness*

One must be ready or one would not recognize the Beloved even if s/he were sitting at the table or knocking at the door. When readiness isn't there, one prematurely excuses oneself from the table or is too busy to answer when the knock comes at the door.

The Beloved has appeared according to plan. But the Lover isn't ready. His heart isn't open enough. His eyes still expect the Beloved to come in a certain form. He is not flexible. He has not given up his pictures of who he thinks the Beloved should be.

But when the Lover is ready, s/he recognizes the Beloved even though the Beloved arrives heavily disguised. You cannot fool the man or woman whose heart is open. S/he looks behind the appearance, sees behind the mask. Attuned to subtle influences, s/he recognizes every clue. S/he is patient and allows things to unfold naturally. There is no rush or push.

Having waited many years for this meeting, what is another day or two? What is another week, or month, or even a year?

What matter if the Beloved's eyes are green instead of brown or her hair is short and curly instead of long and straight? What matter if the Beloved is shorter or taller, bigger or smaller? There is something hauntingly familiar and comfortable about him or her.

The relationship unfolds effortlessly, without deliberation

or struggle. There is no sacrifice here. One gives without worrying if the gift will be returned. One does not hesitate or wait for an accounting.

The Beloved anticipates your need as you anticipate hers or his. That is how lovers dance. They live to give more than to receive, to love more than to be loved.

## *Suffering*

To suffer is to be with *what is,* when *what is* differs from what we want or expect. Since all of us have expectations that are not met, suffering is a normal part of being in relationship.

Most people attempt to escape suffering by trying to change the thinking or the behavior of their partners. This never works. The only thing that can be changed is our own expectations.

When we cease to expect from others what they do not or cannot give to us, our suffering becomes ecstatic. It is transmuted in the fire into submission to *what is.* Resistance is transformed into acceptance.

We learn to submit to the reality at hand without withdrawing our love. We persevere. We persist. We stay present.

It is our gift to our partner: to accept the ragged, unfinished, un-ideal aspects of our union and make the very best of them.

That way we continue to do our part in the relationship.

Even when childhood wounds are triggered, we don't attack our partner or withdraw in anger or frustration. Instead, we admit our fears and trust in our partner's love for us. We rely on the power of love to heal all perceived wounds and deficiencies.

In every relationship, buttons will be pushed and wounds will come up for healing. Every partner has a dark side that s/he is in the process of integrating. Sometimes we will see our partner in the grip of fear. That is why our skillfulness is essential if our relationship is going to weather its storms and trials.

Perhaps that is why we rarely meet our soul mate at a young age. We must learn the necessary relationship skills before we can meet and realize our full potential. For only two skillful, empowered people can give birth to such a mature and transcendent union.

# Requiem

She gave her love to a stranger
who promised her everything.

She mistakenly thought
she could find someone
who could love her more
than she could love herself.

And so by heavenly design
he became a casualty of love
and she the victim
of her own greed.

Dressed in black robes
he learned to preside
over the pageant of boats
that sail out at night
onto the black waters
carrying candles
to commemorate the dead.

There he heard the voices
of his unborn children
warning him that there is no limit
to how many times
the heart can be broken

and urging him
to sink down to a place
beyond sorrow or regret,
where he could honor his pain
and learn from it.

The children taught him
to feel compassion
for those who journeys
were aborted,

for all those creatures
whose legs stalled
at the edge of land,
whose bodies were twisted
and torn in the tides.

Though lame and blind,
battered and broken,
they were willing to trust him
and his pain was the doorway
through which they walked
when morning came.

Though his suffering was small
compared to theirs,
he was the one
through whom truth was spoken
when the stories of the victims
were finally told.

# A Work in Progress

Every relationship is a crucible that builds our strength and increases our capacity for union. Few of us meet the soul mate before dying a thousand deaths in the flames of love. In the process, we awaken to the truth of who we are and who the Beloved is.

Like the Phoenix, we must continually rise from the ashes and learn to trust all over again. If we can keep our hearts open through the disappointments and the betrayals, if we can learn to forgive the trespasses of others as well as our own mistakes, we will emerge from the fire more flexible and resilient, less selfish and stubborn, and more attuned to the subtleties of love.

Each partner who comes to dance with us teaches us something and brings us the gift of connection on one or more levels. Through each, we touch and taste what is possible for us to create with another. In this sense, the soul mate is not just one person, but a work in progress, a tapestry being woven out of light and shadow, hope and fear.

It is a journey of progressive awareness, but it is not a linear one. Often, we come full circle, only to relearn a lesson we could not master before.

Every lover we have prepares us to meet the Beloved. Each one brings a lesson and a gift. And each defers to another who brings a deeper gift and a more compelling lesson.

As we learn to honor ourselves, we attract partners who challenge us to become more conscious about the choices that we make. Gradually, we open our hearts to the potential of creating intimacy on all levels. Life's lessons prepare us for this full-chakra embrace.

In this manner, the way is prepared for the soul mate. When s/he arrives, the way will be straight and clear. There will be no hesitation or confusion.

When the soul mate embraces us, it is no longer a temporal or a temporary affair. It is Spirit come to flesh; it is the indwelling Presence of Love, blessing us and lifting us up. It is both a gift and a responsibility, both a promise made and a promise fulfilled.

# *Mother*

Today I am feeling your pain
and the pain of all the women
who found their voices
after suffering unspeakable acts
of violence and humiliation:
wives who were battered
while their children watched,
mothers who were powerless
to stop the abuse.

Today, I am feeling the pain
of promises made and broken,
betrayals of intimacy and trust.
I am feeling the pain
I have suffered
at the hands of others,
and the pain I have caused
by not knowing who I am
or what I want.

But now those days are over.
I have taken your hand.
I have pressed you to my heart.
Today, I am the bridegroom
sent to the manger
where the holy child is born.
I am the one entrusted
to hold your hand
as you give birth.

*Part Three*

# The Compassionate Heart

*Y*our fingers knit the many colored yarn and pull in the light from all the dark places. For a moment, you are a dreamcatcher, harvesting images that would otherwise be forgotten and consigned to sleep. "See these wonderful hues and shapes," your soft voice hums, "they are your life energy dancing free and clear. You cannot hide it anymore."

My daughter does not know why, but she likes you. It is not hard to like someone when they wrap you in their love, yet hold you ever so lightly. You do not have to give up your freedom to live in the hills and valleys of the Shaman's heart.

You feel the swift harvest of her loss, but do not dwell on it. She wants to know if animals have souls. She wants to know if they can too can be reborn.

Your assurances offer her balm for her wounds. The death of her cat seems to have unleashed the pain she has kept hidden for years. She must take the time to feel that pain and to resurrect it out of the darkness.

I will not let her go into the blackness alone. I will hold a candle and descend into the underworld with her until she feels safe and confident enough to hold that flickering light for herself.

You and I are both keepers of the ferry. We carry our loved ones to the next shore, wherever it is. We need to see them safe on the other side, before we can let them continue on their way along the twisting bend of the river.

Emotional healing is not unlike physical healing. It takes a time for our wounds to heal and for our lives to mend. Yet if we are patient and persistent, healing does happen. There are no orphans in a land of love any more than there is poverty in a land of abundance.

Mother loves her children—every single one of them—completely and without conditions. She cares for them until they are ready to care for themselves. And then she blesses them and lets them go.

# Expirations

*for my father Lindo*

We all tried to deny
the inevitable shift of the tide,
but you chose to stay
and take death
by the hand.

Tucked in
with fresh blankets and sheets,
you closed your eyes
and disappeared
into the rushing waters.

Without hope of a respite,
you pressed on
toward that unknown shore
where the sinking clouds
meet the distant sea,

returning only to take
another raspy and labored breath
that would propel you
further and further
away from us.

Men used to fear
they would fall off
the edge of Earth
if they set sail out beyond
the visible horizon,

but some pushed through that fear
and returned from sea
weathered by wind and waves
to teach us that
wherever we stand

there is always a horizon,
a place beyond the place
where we are,
a land beyond the land
we know.

Maybe this is a metaphor
that applies to this world
and not the next.

Maybe you are right
and there is no afterlife,
no place
where the breath goes
when it leaves the body.

Perhaps, as you did,
we have to accept
the finality of death
without hope of rebirth
or resurrection.

Henry and I watched
as the undertakers
put your lifeless body
in a plastic bag

and lay it like a sack of potatoes
in the van that would take it
to the crematory.

Today all we have of it
is the ashes soon to be scattered
to the wind and waves.

Perhaps I am a fool,
but you do not seem dead to me.

This morning the sun rose
in an explosion of crimson light
behind Thatcher Island.
At 7Am, the light was so intense
you could not look at it.

I had almost forgotten such moments
when the veil opens
and the numinous world
peeks through.

As I walked back
from Good Harbor Beach
everything I looked at was vibrant,
ecstatic, animated and ablaze
with light.

An energy was let loose
in the world,
stirring every hue and shape....
the wind in the brown and orange leaves,
the shadows in the water,

the lion and leopard leaping
from the boulders
on the beach...
everything recessed or hiding
suddenly revealed.

I believe this is the world you inhabit;
not the world of objects,
attachments, or strivings,

but the subtle world
where energies play
and innocently commingle,
transforming all around them.

In this world
death is part of a greater dance,
where many lives come and go,
each keeping its appointed time
without hesitation or protest.

You made your transition
ever so gracefully, going gently
as you went through life.

Today, we celebrate the quiet dignity
of your life and your death.

Today, we claim you
forever in your hearts,
but release you to the wise
and careful course of your journey
wherever it may take you.

Before long each of us
will come to the place
where land ends and sea begins,

and like you we will learn
to trust the tide
to take us out beyond the edge
of what we see or know.

You are there now,
not just there where the sinking sky
meets the swelling sea,
but here among us,

breathing with our breath,
rising and falling with our voices.

If we open deeply,
we can feel you
here beyond the edges
of thought

where form
becomes transparent,
allowing the hidden light
to shine through
full and free.

*Photograph by Anne Rearick*

# Rites of Passage

When my father was dying of cancer, it was not easy for me to see his suffering. Yet it was unavoidable. He had to go through it and my brother and I had to go through it with him. We are both grateful for the last few months we had with him. We are grateful for the smiles and the moments of ecstasy that came in the places left by the pain.

There is a photo that captures one of those ecstatic moments when Isaac, my brother's son, is whispering in my father's ear. Although it was a wordless moment, I hear him saying "Lindo. You are beautiful and I love you. I am so happy to have looked into your eyes, even if it was only for a few precious days, and I am very sad that you are dying. Please don't forget: I will always love you." You can see my father's face totally open and surrendered to that moment. He felt all of that love, innocently and freely given.

I am sure that there were moments of ecstasy like that for Jesus in between the pain, moments when he opened to receive the love of his family and his disciples, moments when he felt the Holy Spirit wrapping his tired and bruised body in Its steady arms. I prefer to remember those moments, rather than the moments of agony on the cross.

I do not deny our pain. How can I? We are all carrying a cross and each one of us suffers on it. But this is only part of the story. The other part must also be told. The times when we trusted, the times when we let go, the times when we opened our hearts to receive the love that was offered to us. Those are the moments we must cherish and remember.

This is the boat that carries us when light fades and the storm comes. These are the oars that row in the darkness and the sail that fills with wind when the rain begins to fall.

# Dream Sequence

Was it a dream
or a moment in time
before the dream began?

In the mother's belly
the child is resting.
She lies on her back
in a canoe

at the edge of a pond,
where light plays
on the leaves of branches
reaching over the water.

Someone has placed her
in this protected place
where they could be launched
into the still, green waters.

Of all the mothers
this one is blessed beyond measure,
kissed by wind,
and caressed by light.

Gently now, the trees bend down
and lift the canoe
into the light strewn waters.

It is a moment
that cannot be captured in time.
The camera falls
from the hands

of the photographer...
and mother and baby go gently
into dark green waters.

There was a time
when we too were carried
by a boat like this one,

as we crossed the river
from that World to this one.

# Part Four

# Ecstatic Energy

*W*hen the energy of love began to embody it provided a whole new experience of intimacy. Every cell of my body was on fire. I felt like the burning bush that Moses met on the way to Mt. Sinai.

The vibration was so intense I thought I would explode. I had to start sharing this energy, because it was impossible for me to contain it. The energy was a gift from the universe. Once received, it had to be given.

When the energy moved through me I would be on fire. When the energy was received by another, s/he would go on fire.

The key to experiencing the transmission of the energy was emotional receptivity. If the recipient was relaxed and open in the heart chakra, the energy would move in easily. If there were blocks there—any kind of fear of love—it would be difficult if not impossible for the energy to enter.

As a general rule, people who functioned in their heads would not feel the energy. The only way that they could experience it would be to relax, stop trying to figure things out, and just be open in the moment.

One thing became clear…very few people were able to embody the energy for very long. That is because they had to stay in a heart-space to continue to embody it. So even if they were sensitive, the energy would diminish when they would go back into their "head space" and become preoccupied by the attempt to function in the world.

The energy could be experienced in the world and in the body, but it was not of the world or the body. The energy was beyond worlds or bodies. It was the energy of love without any conditions.

It was in a very real and visceral sense THE PRESENCE OF LOVE which had taken root in the heart.

In order to receive this energy, the container had to be ready. You had to heal your wounds and open your heart. Then, the love would enter with its fiery flames.

When you embody the energy of love, you become a pure channel, a willing instrument. You exist wholly for the purpose of giving and receiving love.

The more you give the more you receive. And the more you receive the more love you have to give. This is the self-perpetuating engine of divinity at work in you and, through you, in the world.

When love has descended into you in this way, it is hard to have a human lover. It is hard to be in the world and go to a job and be busy with the details of life. It is hard to watch TV or go shopping or do anything that requires us to plan, to think, or to struggle.

It is hard to have sex with someone who is not in their heart. You cannot touch your partner in a mechanical way.

Your need for intimacy and connection becomes deeper and more profound. You require connection on all levels. You require a full-chakra embrace.

When love has taken root in you, there is no outer place where you want to go. You just want to stare into the Beloved's eyes and hold her or him in a never-ending embrace. You want to dwell in the eternal moment. Every cell in your body is connected to every cell in the Beloved's body. Separation dissolves. There is no "I" or "You."

Anything less than this seems unsatisfactory. When love is touching you everywhere from within the outward expression of that love needs to be congruent with what you feeling on the inside. You can't have a partner who is not on fire. S/he won't know what your experience is or how to share it with you.

Yet very few people are embodying this energy and connecting with someone else who is doing it is not something that happens every day. Patience and resolve are necessary.

When you consistently refuse the temptation to accept less than what you are ready to share, the love energy within you begins to draw your soul mate toward you. This is not something that can be intellectually understood. It has to do with the power of resonance or vibration.

You draw to you what is in the same harmonic. Your vibratory rate draws another one like it. You cannot make this happen. It happens by itself. You merely need to cooperate with it.

You do not choose your soul mate. Your soul chooses her or him and draws that person to you when you are ready.

On many levels, the person who comes in may be a

complete mystery to you. Outwardly, s/he might not seem to match any of your pictures or expectations. But inwardly, s/he is completely right and you know it. The vibration and the intensity are there. Others can touch the shell, but s/he can touch the essence. Others are skillful at being in the world. S/he knows how to be in eternity with you. Your shared embrace is a sure sign that heaven has come and made its home in your heart.

# *Fear of Surrender*

Three years ago, I thought that the Beloved had arrived to stay.

S/he came into my life on a long wave. For three months, we both rode that wave until she got scared and ran away. She could touch the eternal moment with me, but she could not submit to it.

I was ready to merge the human world with the divine. She was not. I was ready to surrender, to dissolve into the ocean of love. She was afraid of drowning.

She was afraid of losing herself in me. She did not know that she was entering a different kind of womb, where the ego of both would be left behind so that the butterfly could be born.

The fear of losing self in the process of surrender is very great. For one who has given up her power in the past, this can and must be a red flag.

Only the strong one who is totally guided by her heart can enter this chrysalis with the Beloved. They are pilgrims on a journey to a different place.

The territory has been explored by some. But few have been there. And even fewer still have spoken of it.

# Crucible

This is the crucible
where we bleed a million deaths
and come back to life
almost intact,

the purifying embrace
that hurts in the blood and the bones
turning inside us
like a scythe tilling the fields.

This is the blade
intimate with life and death,
the promise made
only to be broken.

This is the wound
dressed with flowers
and sold at auction
to the highest bidder.

This is the truce made
ever so briefly
between heaven and earth,
male and female, past and future.

This is the dark mystery
of our pain.
blooming like a flower
in the spring rain.

I have met you
in this lifetime and many before.
Now once again
you have turned away.

And I must sit with the sorrow
without expectation
or promise of release.
I must sit face to face

with the one who is still afraid
knowing that she
is but the reflection
of myself.

# *Walking through the Door*

When you told me what you had been feeling for six months, I decided to take the risk and acknowledge that I had been feeling the same energy. But I could not go further than that. Neither one of us was in a position to act on our energetic attraction.

"Let us cultivate our friendship," I told you, "so that there will be some kind of human context around these powerful energies that seem to be erupting in both of us."

In my own obtuse way, I thought it would stop there. I did not know what shenanigans Mother had up her sleeve.

The only physical contact I had had with you was gently taking your hand for a moment. It was innocent enough.

I was still holding all of this at bay. And then you went home and the energy began to embody in you just as powerfully as it had embodied in me some thirty months before. You too began to have a full blown Kundalini experience.

I experienced all this with you. I told you, "The energy is coming through because you are ready to receive it. I am not making it happen."

You did not believe this at first. You thought it was some kind of magic I was doing. You thought that I was somehow seducing you energetically. But I wasn't doing anything. I was just watching it and feeling it with you.

Gradually, you realized you had your own connection to the energy. Even if I were to disappear, that connection would continue. It was a gift from the universe.

Our connection seemed to intensify the energy that we were both feeling. It seemed to amplify it so that it was at least twice as strong for each one of us.

Before you confessed your feelings, the river of love was contained within its banks. But once you acknowledged the truth of your heart, it was only a matter of time before the damn burst and the waters flowed forth, taking everything in their path.

Now we are swimming in those waters. The time and place for love has been ordained by forces greater than us. Our only choice is to submit or not to submit.

# Tapestry

I tried to take you out of me.
It did not work.

I tried to take me out of you;
that failed just as miserably.

We are entwined, intricately knit
into the same tapestry.

I do not have the heart to rip the fabric.
I stand back and admire

what is woven beyond thought
or any meaning we can make.

# *Letters*

*Last night you wrote:*

I need to tell you that I love you. I have been too scared to say it for fear of not knowing what would happen when we are together again, fear that the energy between us would be gone.

I have known it all along, but didn't want to speak it. And also, how could I? I don't even KNOW you. How can you love someone you don't know?

But what if this moment is the only one I have? I want to speak what I am feeling and for you to know. My whole heart feels it. My whole body feels it.

Sometimes it feels so strong that it seems like I may go mad with the intensity of it. So I try to hold it back.

*I wrote:*

I think these words have been hard to speak—the experience is so much bigger than the words—but I am glad you could speak them now, because I know what is behind those words.

*You wrote:*

Thanks for our chat today. Afterwards, I felt such strong energy and warmth return to my entire body.

I went for a walk at sunset during a snowstorm. It was so beautiful. The peace and solitude provided in those woods are amazing. Along my path I met several deer at different times. We would gaze at each other for a few moments and then they would gracefully and quietly leave.

Then I stopped at this wonderful tree. I felt such connection with everything around me. I thought of how we exchange our breath and live from each other.

At one point during my walk, at my favorite part of the path, deep in the cedar bog, I leaned against a tree that was calling to me, and then I felt that wonderful and really intense energy almost immediately upon me.

Yes, I did feel you there. However, I think perhaps you are just the catalyst.

*You wrote:*

I wanted to share this with you before I go. My heart feels so big. That's the only way I can describe it. My ears feel so open. I looked in the mirror and could not believe how flushed my cheeks are. The top of my head feels strange, a tiny bit headachy for a second and then spacious.

While I laid with my kids tonight, I did what you said. While giving my kids hugs, I put my hands on them. They said they didn't feel anything, but my older son said his tummy felt better. I found it a challenge to keep my mind out of it, just pouring love from the heart.

I am still feeling the energy quite a bit; I guess it surprises me every single time I feel it. During my walk today my hands were so cold, but I could feel the energy in my solar plexus and heart, so I stopped, closed my eyes and sent it out to my fingers. All of a sudden my hands warmed. It was amazing. I have been trying to do that for years and now voila.

Is this something that will stay as long as I pay attention to it and stay in my heart, or could it be fleeting? I told you how I felt it so intensely one night for two hours. It was utterly amazing. I felt that night that someone was making energetic love to me. It was totally beyond words and anything I have ever experienced.

So, whatever comes, I am welcoming it and letting it be in charge. Maybe I am dreaming, or losing my grip. It seems to be getting stronger. Today I had to undo my bra because it felt so tight across my chest, right at the nipple line—that's the heart chakra.

I am feeling so blessed for this opportunity to feel any of this. I don't understand it, but I'll be here for it as long as it is here.

*You wrote:*

As I laid in bed last night, I thought I felt you, then I wasn't sure. I am always feeling the buzzing, electric sensation. I am assuming that is the life force energy. Then I can feel heat. I also get a physical sensation in my 1st/2nd chakra/pelvic area. It's almost like the opening up that I feel in my heart—that expansive, yet relaxed feeling.

Maybe none of these sensations are from you. Last night I wanted to feel you, but then thought maybe I'm just alone here and making it up.

Yet today the energy was *really* strong after I talked to you and stayed until I jumped into my head. I am noticing how it is affected by what I am feeling in my heart.

*You wrote:*

I just got back from an awesome walk. I needed to be alone so I drove to a park nearby with many trails. I picked a trail I've never been on before and set out, even though it was dusk. It was so beautiful. The snow was blanketing the ground and fallen trees. It was totally quiet and I was completely alone. By the time I was half way around the trail it was dark. I couldn't even see the path in front of me because it was all white and it was more than a little eerie. So I made it a fun exercise in trusting myself and the universe. I drove home the long way around and saw nine deer and a beautiful, magnificent moon with just a sliver lit up!

Last night, for an hour and a half, I felt that I was receiving this energy from you. I guess I wanted to know if you were feeling it too or if I was alone in my own little moment of ecstasy. Was that something shared or something I created on my own?

Of course, when I feel my heart, I feel you. So, I try to stay out of my head so I can meet you in the heart. Yes. I want an ecstatic union too, but I have been scared to put it into words. I haven't been in that space for at least a decade and I have never shared it with someone. So you are giving me this space to explore it, walk around in it, swim in it, bathe in it, rest in it. It is very wonderful and healing.

I feel like a warrior, returning from battle, letting all his armor and weapons fall off, as he approaches home.

Part of me is scared though. Like those deer in the park. The humans they encounter there won't hurt them. But what if they venture out of the park? Outside the park there are humans who may not be so kind and loving toward them.

I was going to keep this to myself, but I really want to share it with you. I was listening to a CD in the car and the workshop leader was talking about the heart and how we need to be married to ourselves but usually seek relationships to give our hearts what they need. But then she said, "When you find a life partner, it's not because you are afraid to go into your heart. It's because you've been there and you know what it needs." I almost fell off my chair when I heard that. And yes, I do have a *knowing* of what I want and need. I feel like I have known all along, but for some reason wouldn't admit it.

*You wrote:*

All day yesterday I felt like a stranger in my home. Everything felt awkward.

Sometimes I think that maybe I want to run to you to get away from the ordinary, mundane aspects of life. But then I get that feeling through me like you have just completely entered the inside of my body. That is not something I have ever felt before. I feel like if I could feel that more often I could love anyone and that they could stay as long as they wanted—that total bliss. What is this all about? Do you think I am a crazy?

# Loons

Yes, you are a crazy loon.
There's just no way around it.

On my lake in New Hampshire this summer,
I saw two loons, a male and female, a couple.

They were swimming near each other,
but there was a powerful energy connecting them.

They were the keepers of the lake.
Perhaps that is what we are.

*Part Five*

# Freedom and Devotion

*W*hen I think about the quality of our love for each other, several things stand out. The first is safety. We both feel safe and at home in each other's presence. It has always been like that for the two years that we have known each other as friends.

It is not surprising then that the feeling of safety continues at the physical level and that our bodies feel best when they are next to each other. This has nothing to do with sexuality. It is the Mother energy that holds us and in which we hold each other. Its touch is gentle and reverent. Its feeling is profound closeness.

It easily moves into lovemaking, because it is filled with love and wants to express love in any way that pleases the Beloved. But it is also content just being present, hand in hand, breathing together. When I lay my head against your chest, you are both lover and mother and this allows me to sink into you deeply and profoundly. It enables me to experience an intense sense of connection and belonging.

So too when you come into my arms, I am both your lover who embraces you and your father who protects you. You lean on me and allow me to support you. I can feel you sinking into me and feeling my strength. I know that you feel safe with me and free to be yourself.

These are not deliberate gifts that we give to one another. They are spontaneous and unrehearsed. They are simply how our energies play and merge together. We do not do anything to make this happen. We are simply present and the dance begins.

Indeed, we can't understand how any of it happens. It just does. It gathers us up and begins to move us in and through each other.

In the dance of life, obstacles arise and we dance around them. Sometimes we approach them gently and they simply dissolve, yielding to the intensity of our love. We begin to realize that some things are simply ordained to happen. They cannot be anticipated or planned. They cannot be engineered, provoked, or prodded, even by prayer. The Tao—the rhythm of life—cannot be scripted. It unfolds only in the present moment.

Of course, we try to study love—to see what works and what doesn't—to learn from our own mistakes and the mistakes of others. But it doesn't seem to matter. We make the same mistakes over and over again. Until one day, we do something just a tiny bit different, without knowing how or why. And everything shifts. Everything changes.

The way we became lovers was like that. We simply spoke the words that were in our hearts. We were completely innocent and trusting. And suddenly and without effort our bodies were completely immersed and we were swimming in the river, its swift current pulling us downstream.

Once you are in the river, you cannot argue with it. You cannot step back and analyze it. You cannot ask "Is this good for me?" or "Will I be safe?" You just need to keep moving your arms and legs.

In the river, the conceptual mind is barely useful and practically irrelevant. To stay in the river of love, you have to trust the current, even though you don't know where it is taking you. You have to surrender, to be okay with not knowing.

Love for the Beloved happens only now in this moment. This is the river. It is always moving, never static. It requires from us only to be present, to be aware, to be willing.

You cannot anticipate what the Beloved will need or know how you will meet that need any more than you can anticipate and know how to meet your own needs. Life is constant motion. Needs are perpetually shifting and changing.

The river is always unpredictable. Sometimes it flows peacefully in the moonlight. And sometimes the wind picks up and waves dance madly, catching the sunlight as they hit the rocks, spawning countless rainbows.

Love is also unpredictable. Do you think you can know what you need or what the Beloved needs? No, it is not possible, any more than it is possible for the river to stay calm when the wind picks up.

All is energy. All is movement. All is surrender.

Love needs this freedom and devotion in every moment or its dance will end. Resist the movement of water and wind, and you will emerge from the river tired and bruised. Such is the likely end of any love in which the lovers attempt to direct or take control.

So we must learn to breathe now as we swim even though our heads occasionally go under water. We must learn to blow the water out of our mouths and catch our breath just in time. We must learn how to handle the unexpected challenges and the moments when we are pushed beyond our comfort zone.

True lovers learn to do the dance that love asks them to do, because they know that they have no choice. They cannot stop their love any more than they could begin it.

Love is and will always be a mystery. We do not know how it comes and goes. Beginnings and endings—if they exist at all—are not up to us.

Some people do not understand. They think they get to say "Yes" or "No" to the call of love. They are completely deluded. No one who has ever loved deeply and truly has ever had such a choice.

# Drinking the Elixir

We were born in different parts of the world.
and had many lives to live
before we were ready to surrender
completely to each other.

But now all that has changed.

Ever since the solstice came
and the dark days of winter
yielded to the days of waxing light
I have lived and breathed in your orbit.

Winter's momentum has been broken
and the seed energy of spring
is taking root in our lives.

Wherever I go now, you are there,
shimmering all around me,
like lights flickering in the dark waters
when the wind picks up.

Lovers live in an altered state
in which mysteries and paradoxes abound.

Life is no longer perceived as it used to be.
It is spontaneous and unpredictable,
like the flower in your garden
blooming in the snow on the day we met.

Sun and moon may appear to be different,
but they are connected at the deepest level.
No coin has only one side.

The opposites mutually arise
and all of manifest existence
is merely the spontaneous expression
of their playful dance.

Light and darkness do not exist
in separate worlds,
but in one unbroken continuum.
How else could we meet?

Without this intrinsic harmony
within the dualistic structure of life,
our union would exist only
as some untapped potential,

some beauty conceived in the heart
never to be spoken by the lips
nor touched by human hands.

Neither one of us would accept this fate.
That is why we cannot allow our lives to be defined
by narrow ideas or earthly logic.

The stars obey laws we have not heard of yet
and cannot possibly understand.

Love may be blind, yet only those who love
understand that the very planet we live on
comes from the mysterious union of
two heavenly bodies.

It is conceived in the union of their mutual love,
and born as a perfect balance
between male and female,
mind and heart, body and soul.

Such is the chemistry of fate.
We can experience it, but we can never explain it.

That is why you and I will raise this goblet to our lips
and drink until we have quenched our thirst.
What choice do have we?

No one who has lived has not loved.
No one who has been offered the elixir
has refused to drink it.

# *Full Immersion*

We are all so afraid of losing control. Yet there is no control to be had. Control is a conceit of the ego. It perpetuates the false belief and expectation that things will show up the way we want them to. Usually that doesn't happen.

Yet when it does, it can only be because we are clear about what we want and willing to surrender our expectations of how our needs will be met. Instead, we trust the process and allow our lives to unfold with their own inner rhythm and purpose. And then, from time to time, miracles do happen.

The universe cooperates with us and supports us in moving forward into our greater growth and increasing capacity to love and to serve. Sometimes our needs are met in the nick of time just when we are beginning to despair. And sometimes, our hunger is intuited before we even become aware of it, and the universe brings our dinner in fully cooked on the most amazing hand-painted plates, served with the finest wine.

Could we recreate the moment if we wanted to? It is very unlikely. Our only choice is to open our arms and accept the gift when it is offered to us.

Many people ask me "What can I do to bring the Beloved in?" It is amazing to me how people can even ask that question. How else would you meet the Beloved except by following the desire of your heart? There is no other way.

Do you really think it is possible to find love by cutting off your passion? Do you really think there is some higher form of love apart from the yearning of the heart or the rhythms of the body? No. That is not love. That is not devotion.

Love cannot be engineered. It can only be discovered. And once we have discovered it and opened our hearts to it, we know that it is a gift from the universe. Had we looked for it with our discriminating minds, we never would have found it. It could come to us only because our hearts were open.

Love is so much more powerful than anything the mind can muster. Just one look from the Beloved's eyes will undermine the most carefully laid plans. Just one touch of her hand will take down all your vows of celibacy.

Love asks only one thing of us. It asks us to let go. It asks us to trust. If there is anything that you are holding onto, you cannot love.

Love and control are not congruent. That is why to love, you must lose this mind that wants to control, to shape your destiny, to know in advance, to have probabilities, if not guarantees. No, you cannot love with the mind. You have to sink into the heart.

Those who are not in love think that lovers are crazy and of course they are. They have let their minds go. There is nothing rational about what they say or do. They do not act in a way that protects themselves. They are like wolves howling during a harvest moon. They are absolutely crazed.

Lunacy is not some made-up disease. Every lover has it. He is condemned to lose himself totally in the Beloved. He does not even know that he has a separate mind or body.

What is this dance that lovers do that ignores the boundaries and limits of our conventional world? Some say it is just pure foolishness and that the lovers will wake from their dream ashamed of themselves.

But the true lover is already awake. His ego has vanished —temporarily perhaps—but vanished nonetheless. The Lover lives only to serve and to please the Beloved. He cannot do this when he holds himself apart from her in any way.

So he dives into the river. He lets go and takes the plunge into the unknown. Without protecting himself, without deliberating or considering his options, he leaps from the banks of the stream and lets the waters embrace him.

This is a form of baptism very few clergy know about. When we no longer resist any part of ourselves and there is nothing that we withhold from the Beloved, we move beyond any possibility of sin or shame to discover our true innocence in and around the body. Indeed, to lie next to the Beloved is the holiest of acts. It is where the body becomes fully consecrated and placed in the service of love and devotion.

No, it is not that the Lover must wake up from his dream of immersion. Quite the contrary, he must enter the dream fully awake. He must participate fully and consciously in the dance.

One does not enter the dance to leave it. One enters the dance to surrender completely, and to become the very presence of love itself. The Beloved is but the doorway and with her help, the Lover can cross the threshold that separates self from other.

This is not a worldly act, but an act of intense spiritual devotion. There is nothing ordinary or pedestrian about it. Nor is it "holy" in some conventional way, for it moves without a mask or an agenda. It is poetry in motion—an inner unfolding of scripture from the heart to the lips—so that we hear the words as if they were spoken for the first time.

If love has cast a spell upon the Lover and the Beloved, then it is a necessary spell. All who come into the gravitational field of the lovers are themselves at risk of going mad. This, my friends, is a disease that has no cure.

Some say they do not know where the river begins. I say, it begins where you jump in. And then it has no end until it reaches the sea.

# *Lowering the Bucket*

It seems strange to both of us that we are unable to be more than several feet away from each other without gravitating back into each other's arms. We thought that this would end in a few days or weeks, but in fact it has become even more intense.

The heart aches if it strays from this embrace and then the aching pulls it back again and again. Sometimes it seems there is a new heart being born from our two hearts. And this heart also has its openings and closings, its rhythmic diastole, its intense pull in and out like the tides.

We live in separate bodies, but now those bodies are becoming more transparent. The mystery of the shared heart and the ecstatic urge to merge—as futile as the attempt may be—cannot be resisted. Our embrace continues to deepen in intensity until our shared energy body has been created. That is the angelic container of our relationship.

When we rest fully in that body, our joining is complete. Even when we are physically separated we do not feel apart, but remain in soul-union. Love now exists beyond time and space. It exists both in the body and outside it.

The opportunity to love in this way arises from the intense desire for union and the capacity to submit to it. If this is mutual, then the pathway to the Beloved unfolds in this world and in this life.

Yet as long as there is stored pain and resentment from the past, the pathway will not open. True lovers must be ready to be all and to give all. They mast take the time needed to heal their wounds so that their hearts can be open. Only then can the bucket be lowered into the well. Only then can the Beloved's thirst be quenched when she arrives from her long and circuitous journey.

# *The First Supper*

I live in your heart. You simply need to be aware of me to know that we are not separate. I am not here across the ocean from you. Every time you take a breath, I am like the air that moves in and out of your lungs. Every time your heart beats, I am like the blood that moves though your veins.

You and I are not separate any more than the moon is separate from the sun or the earth separate from the moon. We live in perpetual relationship to one another, constantly shining and reflecting each other. Our orbits are perfectly placed for giving and receiving. We need merely follow their appointed course.

It is said "What God has brought together, no one can pull apart," and so it is for us. We did not bring ourselves to this table of abundance. We were brought here by forces far beyond our understanding or control.

You knocked on the front door of the house, not knowing that I was knocking at the rear door. Each one of us arrived separately and was welcomed in kind. It was not until we sat across from each other at the dinner table that we understood our divine appointment.

Had we known what was coming, we might have hesitated or arrived before it was time for our meeting. But because we did not know, we could learn to trust our guidance and follow a pace that was comfortable for each of us.

Had our egos taken charge of this meeting, it might not have happened. Or, if it did, it might have been completely botched.

Let us be glad that we innocently made our way to this place. And let us also be grateful that when the veil was removed we were able to see deeply into each other's eyes.

For it is not enough for Lover and Beloved to be drawn together. They must also open their eyes and recognize each other.

# Tree of Life

*There is no escape from this embrace.*
*We are entwined together like the branches on the tree of life.*

Some would say that it was destiny that brought us together. But was it not also free will? Did we not also decide what was most important for us and move toward it, however awkwardly? Did we not fall many times in the darkness and pick ourselves up off the ground, holding a vision of light, even as we moved through the shadowy realm?

Without a vision of the Beloved, the Lover is stranded in a world that he does not like or understand. He is marooned on a sterile island, surrounded by fierce winds and stormy seas. But with a vision of the Beloved, he is given a boat and a compass. He can leave behind that isolated island and set sail for a place he knows in his heart but is not yet able to see.

He will have many challenges along the way. He will weather vicious storms in which he almost loses hope of ever seeing land. And he will breathe a sigh of rlief when the storms subside and the clouds open at the horizon, revealing a sunrise of unsurpassed beauty.

And then one day, unexpectedly, he will look out over the waters and see the thin outline of mountains on the horizon. And he will feel a stirring in his heart that feels deeply familiar as he approaches the shoreline and enters the harbor.

When at last he anchors his boat and swims ashore, there is no doubt in his mind that he has arrived home. Without difficulty, he finds the path that leads to the top of the mountain and builds a great bonfire to celebrate his arrival. He has total certainty now, for his vision has finally been fulfilled.

You have asked me how I too can so quickly ascend the mountaintop. Perhaps it is because I have spent so many days at the base of the mountain, exploring every rocky footpath. I know every twist and turn of the path. Even at night, the light from the crescent moon is sufficient to guide my footsteps.

Certainty comes from the depth of the heart. It is rooted deeply and is not swayed by the winds of doubt or fear. It rests in itself. It knows without knowing how it knows.

That is how the Lover recognizes the Beloved and understands that his vision has been fulfilled. It is not something that can be explained to others. The Beloved submits to that certainty, even though she knows not from whence it comes or where it goes.

She too is completely unprepared for this. Yet she is totally taken. Her body holds all of him inside her now. They rest in each other's arms now as if they have rested there throughout eternity.

Those who pass by them see a single tree, not two trees whose branches are entwined. And that tree has a profound reach and a canopy that shelters all who pass under it.

# Coming Home

Where we are from
is also where we are going.

Had we known this before we departed
we might not have taken the journey.

But not knowing it
we decided to venture forth

seeking something
we did not believe we had

some missing Grail
we had to find.

After many detours and cul-de-sacs,
we gave up the search

accepting ourselves as we are,
and then it no longer mattered

which direction we took
because it became clear

that all roads
lead to the same place.

Now we see clearly
what at the beginning

was just a fog,
for we have removed the dark glasses

from our eyes
and have come face to face.

This destination is also the place
where our journey began.

Perhaps we had to leave home
to find our way back there.

Perhaps not.
Perhaps the journey itself is imaginary.

Perhaps there is no end
and no beginning,

just this moment
without beginning or end.

Perhaps there is no Lover,
no Beloved,

no male or female,
no you or me,

just this all-encompassing love
at home in Itself.

# The Dance of Love

Life has humbled him.
His tough and obstinate heart
has been softened
and made more resilient.

His capacity to love
has been tested and purified.
The needs of the Beloved
have become as important as his own.

He has learned that
the greatest gift he can give her
is to be himself
and to allow her to be herself.

He has learned that
only with that freedom
and that permission
can the dance of love begin.

# Part Six

# Lilies of the Field

We humans are addicted to struggle. We do not believe that we can earn a living without hard work, sacrifice and suffering. We have subscribed to this sad, tedious epic of self-betrayal in the name of God, or country or family. Take your choice.

Yet work does not make us happy, any more than sex does or money does. Happiness does not come from anything a human being can do. It comes from within a human being, usually when he is not preoccupied with himself.

Love and happiness have the same source. They arise in the heart when the heart is at peace with itself and others. Then a human being can bloom like a flower.

Yes, it is true. We must learn to relax. We must take a deep breath and come back into our bodies. We cannot be in the hectic pace of life and be connected to our hearts, to the source of our happiness and our love.

We need to sink in and feel our roots. After all, that is how the flower grows. It blooms from the bottom up, not from the top down.

Yet human life is so top-heavy. The head weighs down on the body like a huge boulder. Is it any wonder that our shoulders are crushed and our necks are out of alignment? Tension, muscle tightness, and a back that is twisted in pain is the mark of modern life. Just touch anyone and you can feel rocks in the places where feathers should be.

People talk about angels without understanding that they are called to grow wings in this life. But wings do not come to one who holds the world up like Atlas. We need to put the world down, in more ways than one.

What are you doing that you believe that you have to do? In what area of life do you believe you have to sacrifice? Where do you believe you have no choice? That is where your tension lives. That is where your self betrayal originates.

Please take a breath and realize that "no choice" is a belief that Atlas has to have, because without this belief he could not justify his job description or the pain in his shoulders. Without this belief, he could let the world drop from his shoulders and take a walk in the woods or a swim in the stream.

Atlas is no longer Atlas without this belief. He is no longer responsible for the world. He is no longer locked into the role of caretaker or savior. He can just be a simple human being.

People who try to be Gods quickly become sub-human. Their animal nature is ignored or transgressed. Desires become unconscious. Anger and fear are submerged. The body cries out for recognition, but its cries are ignored.

This is not the way to Angelhood, but the way to hell on earth, as the Devil can attest. Only when we stop trying to be

Gods do we have the hope of being human, and only when we have become fully human do we have the possibility of growing our wings.

Anyone who cannot live in acceptance and forgiveness of himself or others still has rocks in the places where his wings would grow. He desperately needs to breathe. He needs to stop trying so hard to prove his worthiness.

All this is shame-driven. It is completely futile. None of us will ever prove that we are worthy of love. This is not something that can be proved, especially when you don't believe it.

Self worth does not come from the mind or any thinking process. It is completely existential. It comes with the breath or the breath has already been psychologically compromised.

Human beings need a yoga of the heart that re-connects the mind and body, that re-joins our desire to our purpose, and makes room for our joy to gather and express itself. There is a Tao—a river of life—that flows in our body/mind/spirit container. There is prana, life energy, the cultivation of which leads to spontaneity and grace. When the Tao flowers in our hearts it joins us intimately to the wind and the moon and the trees, to the whole manifest universe.

Only the mind can hold us apart from life. That mind has become preoccupied and self-absorbed. It forgets to move or to breathe. It loses touch with its existential roots, its joy, its spontaneous connection to life. And without that connection to life, trust in self or others is not possible. The connection to the divine is truncated, ripped like an umbilical cord from the baby before it is ready to separate from the mother.

It seems that human beings have forgotten how to nurture

themselves or their offspring. They are at war with their bodies and with the world they live in.

They live in a high state of stress, poorly managed by drugs that pummel the body into submission. No, this is not the way of living that the Master told us about in the Sermon on the Mount. This is a travesty. This is human life become contorted, twisted, demonic. Love and trust have no place in such a life.

Atlas guards the doorway through which the messenger would come. He will not let him enter. There will be no John the Baptist or redeemer now. There are just inmates and guards in the prison we keep creating. No way in and no way out.

If we want the walls of this prison to fall, we must learn to breathe, each of us alone, and then all together, like the wolf that blew down the pig's house. And I have news for you. One wolf is not going to do it. It will take a whole pack of wolves, because this prison we have built is not made only of wounds and false beliefs; it is built with bricks and mortar.

That is the measure of human civilization I'm afraid. If it is not made of asphalt, it is made of concrete and steel. There is a heaviness that looms over the world. Human creations weigh down heavily on the shoulders of Mother Earth. And She is not Atlas. She does not even pretend to be. Unless we want to kill the Great Mother, we will have to slow the pace of our mad creations and learn to breathe and connect with the Planet Earth again. All of the indigenous peoples know this. But we are not asking them.

We have developed an antagonistic relationship with the

very planet that gives us life. We are a long way, dear Jesus, from the lilies of the field.

We have forgotten the laws of love. I wonder, "Did we ever know them? Did we ever know that we are one with God, equal to our brothers and sisters, and responsible for our creations? Did we ever understand the expression *Thy will be done?*"

No it is not the Father's will nor the Mother's that prevails on this shaking orb, coughing and spitting as it flies through the black interstellar spaces. Nor is this Armageddon—the battle in the skies for the souls of women and men—or if it is—T.S. Elliot was right and Earth is sickly and wobbling seriously now. There is no telling how long it will hobble and stutter before its legs give out and its voices are silenced, before its engine sputters and goes out "not with a bang, but with a whimper."

I do not mean to alarm or depress. The media do a better job of that than I could do. I speak simply with the voice of the withered flower, whose roots are shallow and dry. I do not think her tiny voice will be heard. Indeed, I would be surprised if anyone was listening.

# *Stolen Hearts*

Looking into your eyes
I die a thousand deaths.

We have grown old together
and forgotten the moment

when we saw each other
for the first time.

It is a sad time.
People perish inside such lapses

of the heart.
Some are lost forever.

No matter how hard we look
we cannot dig them up

or revive them.
They have gone into a world

we will never know.
They have disappeared

and taken our hearts
with them.

# The Riddle of the Sphinx

### I

They say that Oedipus
did not want to kill his father
or marry his mother.

They say that was some kind of fate.
But I do not believe it.
It was not fate.
It was not destiny.

It was just what happens when a man tries
to run away from what he is afraid of.
I say: face that fear.
Look at it.

We all have mother and father wounds.
Like Oedipus, some of us
even act them out.

We can't heal our pain
unless we know the extent of the wound
and have the courage to face it.

We can't heal if we must put out our eyes
because we are afraid to see the truth.


## II


Your spiritual teacher
sees the death of the ego
in Oedipus' self mutilation.

But to me this is not ego death,
but the terrible price of denial.

To equate acts of self mutilation
with spiritual growth
is to deny the legitimate needs

of body and soul
and make a mockery of both.

It merely reinforces
the schizophrenic division
between sexuality and spirituality
endemic to the western mind.

I prefer a different metaphor
for spiritual growth.
After all sex is not evil
and austerities are not a measure of faith.

The body does not stand in the way of truth;
but merely gives us the opportunity
to discover it in us and around us.

Ask the Sphinx.
He does not fight against
his animal nature,
but wholeheartedly embraces it.

Only those who strive to be immortal
need to be afraid of their desires.

The rest of us are content
to find heaven here on earth
where life is often fragile
and undefended.

## III

In the end Oedipus must learn
that gouging out his eyes
does not heal the wound,
but only exacerbates it.

Self mutilation may be
an expression
of guilt or regret
but it is not an act of atonement.

Oedipus will not be released from his pain
until he learns to forgive
his father and his mother
and most of all himself.

Only then will those piecing blue eyes
torn from their sockets
be restored
to their rightful place.

The windows to the soul
shut up through acts of terror
on the body
must be re-opened.

Light must be let in
to the dark places within the soul.

That is the only way
that integration can happen

and light no longer separate
from the darkness
can blend with and illumine it.

Then even blind Tiresias
can regain his sight,
for knowledge will come

not with the sharp blade
of guilt and punishment

but with the gentle embrace
of compassion and forgiveness.

IV

Thus the drama comes to an end
and the actors return home
with poignant memories
of the characters they played.

Wounds heal.
Daggers are withdrawn
and placed on the altar
for a final blessing.

The bells of the temple
toll for you and me
and all the others
who temporarily lost their way
on planet Earth.

And an octave higher
we hear the sound of Krishna's flute
leading us back to a place
that feels safe and familiar.

In this place
all of us are innocent.
All of us are accepted and loved.
All of us are forgiven.

# *Tears*

You have written a story about a woman whose name is Tears. She knows what everyone knows but is afraid to admit. She lives in a deep sadness. She is tired and her body is limp.

Tears is you, yet you are more than her.

You are like the captain of a small boat that has come through a tempest with damaged mast and torn sails. You have arrived in this safe harbor, your mind edgy, your body battered and bruised, your spirit shaken. You have weathered the storms of love and yes, they have taken their toll.

I see this in your eyes. I feel the pain of the abandoned little girl within you, the one who just wanted to be loved by her mommy, but was beaten instead. Life has not been kind to you, yet you have survived. You have found a way to love yourself against all odds.

You see, my dear, you have learned something few people learn. You have learned to rely on yourself.

Of course, in the beginning you hoped that your knight would show up and carry you across the stormy waters. But each time you yielded the helm to another, the storms deepened and you paid the price. In the end, you accepted the need to sail alone. You understood that no one else could bring you to the safe harbor where you could rest and rebuild your life.

Now finally, you must give yourself space and time to heal. Drink in the warm sun that shines on you. Leave the cold mountains and the harsh winds behind. Your days of working like a slave and fighting for your life are over. There is a lifetime of striving and abuse that needs to come to an end.

Let the memories and the dreams come up. Write them down. Let the waves of emotion you have been holding inside come spilling out. Stop holding all this back. Let the dam burst.

It is time for you to cry the ocean of tears you have been holding inside. It is time for you to let your body shake with hopelessness and hidden grief. Please, hold nothing back. Let go of everything.

Here you are safe. Here you can cry until there are no tears left. Yes, be Tears now. Be her completely.

There will come a time when Tears will disappear into the ocean of your grief and the ocean will carry her. It will no longer be your job to hold onto her. You will let her go into the ocean of sadness that holds all pain and regret. You will release her to the great suffering heart of the mother who could not love you or herself.

It is time to know and to trust that in our pain, we are healed. In our sadness we are uplifted. In the death of our False Self, we are resurrected to a new and better life.

We are told by the Preacher "there is a time for everything...a time to be born and a time to die, a time to plant and a time to reap, a time to be wounded and a time to heal."

This is the time ordained for healing. The search has been long and deep, but it has ended now. The stones that have been gathered must be scattered to the winds.

This is not a time to embrace, but a time to refrain from

embracing. What has been torn must be mended now.

There will come a time for love once again, for everything has its season. But now is not the time for love.

Now is the time for the Self to be born, for the light to be found in the darkness, for the truth to be spoken in the silence of the heart.

# The Choice

There comes a time when he must choose.
For he has two soul mates, not one.

One he can live with.
The other he cannot live with.

One shares his bed and his room.
The other has her own bed and her own room.

One comes and goes as she pleases.
The other one never leaves his side.

One comes to him to learn to shine on her own.
The other one is content to reflect his light.

One inspires him and delights in his creations.
The other one listens to him and holds him when he cries.

He knows he must choose carefully
for the one he chooses will accompany him
for the rest of his life.

Somehow all this has happened before.

The one who vies with him will win the match
but she will lose him in the end.

Strangely enough, this does not bother her.

*Part Seven*

# Radical Acceptance

*M*any of us have the fantasy that the soul mate is going to solve all problems, heal all wounds, and love us exactly as we would like to be loved. If we do not surrender the fantasy, it will become a cross on which our relationship will be crucified over and over again.

To realize the truth of our relationship we must let go of our need to have a perfect partner or to be perfect for our partner. Only the ego requires perfection, and no ego can ever be perfect for another ego. The ego must be surrendered for the reality of the soul connection to materialize.

Our partner challenges us in every moment to accept him or her as s/he is now, not as s/he used to be in the past, or as we would have him or her be in the future. We must offer each other radical acceptance moment to moment or our soul connection cannot be accessed. And without that connection, our partnership will lack energy and purpose. It will lose its sacredness and become profane.

# Sacred Partnership

The focus of the first part of our journey is individual and personal. It is about claiming our right to be ourselves. It is about making our own choices and taking responsibility for them. When our personal empowerment work is done, we become a potential equal of another human being. We are ready to walk through life with a friend, a companion, a lover, a mate.

At this stage of the journey we do not have to worry about giving our power away. We know that we cannot and will not do that. We are content now to bring our own gift and welcome the gift the other person brings.

Only two very strong individuals who are certain of their equality can create such a union. If either one feels insecure or unworthy, s/he will be unable to be fully present and responsible and the capacity of the partners to create an equal partnership will be compromised.

In order for sacred partnership to evolve, both people must really want equality and be devoted to creating it. This devotion is the gift each person brings to the relationship. It cannot be demanded, negotiated or bartered for. It is either given freely and completely, or it is not given at all.

# *Deepening*

When we submit to our relationship the way it is, we begin to uncover the hidden treasures of our union. We remove our masks and see the real person who lives and moves beneath it. We become visible and vulnerable to each other. We connect in our nakedness, essence to essence. We meet where we breathe together, where our thoughts and feelings originate, where our hearts open and close.

This is just the beginning of our experience together. In the alchemical fire, thoughts must constellate and become truth. Feelings must become congruent and become acceptance and love.

In the heat of the alchemical fire, the boundaries between self and other must be dissolved. "I" must be transmuted into "We." Two must become one.

Only two people who have individuated can do this. Those who have not yet come into their power must continue to set limits and hold onto their boundaries so that they will not slip back into co-dependency. They must focus on the "I" because they have too easily betrayed themselves in the past.

But true lovers must go beyond limits and boundaries. They must go beyond the "I" without abandoning it. They must explore the "We" and allow the "I" to find its place within a larger consciousness and experience.

The soul mate brings the invitation to this third phase of

the Lover's journey. The first phase is for family and child rearing. The second part is for individuation. And the third part is for love and surrender.

Without the Beloved, the "We" cannot be complete. S/he is the midwife for this transformational work, in which selfish love dies and is reborn as love without conditions.

Lover and Beloved are growing together in a chrysalis, like a caterpillar in a cocoon. The wings of the butterfly are taking color and shape in the dark, transformational womb. If those wings are going to emerge safely from the chrysalis, patience and trust are necessary.

# Transfiguration

The Lover without the Beloved
is like the sky without the ground,
like a boat without a rudder,
wandering about aimlessly,
buffeted by the winds
pulled in and out at will by the tides.

But when the Beloved arrives
in the autumn of life,
the engine of purpose is lit.
The forest brightens.
Gold and crimson leaves
stand out in their fullness and purity.

Minds learn to trust
and bodies to surrender.
Two bright flames
once burning separately
now dissolve into one steady light,
one love, one heart, one eternal embrace.

# *Emergence*

*for my daughter Arianna*

I know you think you came to earth
to suffer and die.

For years you tried
to hide your pain
and when you could not hide it
you tried to resist
this dire birth into life.

Meanwhile the fire rages
on the mountainside
and you are powerless to change
the degree or course
of its devastation.

You are right to await your time.
Even the flood of tears
you stoically hold back
could not fill a single bucket
to hurl against the flames.

Yet I know and one day so will you
that the fire has its purpose
and all who suffer the flames
are transformed by them
willingly or not.

For years you carried your pain.
Now it carries you.

Now you hear the muffled
and unsteady sound of life
rumbling inside you.
Now you hear the troubled voice
vibrating in your heart.

It can no longer be silent.

No matter how hard you resist,
the poem of your pain
will rise to your lips,
and you will tremble like a leaf,
in a cold night wind

Birth is a sudden
and unpredictable thing.
For many nights nothing happens
and then one night
your heart splits open

and your soul stirs from its long sleep,
lifting you out of night
into this fiery morning
like the Phoenix
rising from its ashes.

One night a little girl's shame
is consumed in the flames
revealing her innocence
and her torn, bleeding body
is resurrected in the crimson sky.

The pain and trauma of the past
are finally forgiven
and fade with the cold night wind
moving away from land
out over the waters.

In the aftermath of the storm
the sea is calm.
There are no boats to be seen.
Just the sky reflected
in the deep blue waters.

# The Master Teacher

You are not like other women. They do not know how to hold the space for the Beloved. But you know. You have waited for me patiently for many years. Even after I came into your life, you waited. You waited until the words that needed to be spoken could no longer be withheld. You waited until the arms of friendship deepened into the arms of love.

My tree at the De Soto Monument is like that. Its branches extend fully and gracefully in all directions. It dances with the sky and with the ground, delighting in its relationship to both.

When you meet this tree it literally takes your breath away. You have to remember to breathe. You have to remember that you too are an intermediary between heaven and earth. You have to bring the breath down into your roots and sink them deeply in the ground. Only when you are rooted in this way, can you appreciate the power and purpose of this tree.

My tree is a poem in the making. Whitman and Rumi would understand it.

A tree like this does not need a lover. It is its own lover. It embodies both male and female, root and branch, sky and ground. It fully expresses itself yet shelters you like a great mother.

Children go crazy when they see this tree. They cannot keep themselves away from it. It is completely approachable. It invites them into its branches as a woman invites her babies to nurse at her breasts. Adults stop in their tracks and behold the tree's magnificence. Some stare for hours, involved in some silent reverie or mystical experience.

This tree is a symbol of what love can be when it is fully empowered and free to be itself. Lovers who behold each other in this way are already resting in the Beloved's arms.

This is not something you can teach someone to do. It is just something that happens when you are ready. Real love cannot be learned or taught. It cannot be engineered or brought into manifestation. It has its own inner rhythms that must find their true expression.

Authenticity is not learned. It is indwelling. It is organic. To find it, we must accept and learn to trust who we are.

It seems ironic, but just by being ourselves we make the greatest contribution possible to the common good, because we show all who come our way what is possible for them. Like Jesus or Buddha, we model the state of total freedom and acceptance.

The great challenge for human beings is to integrate their sexuality with their spirituality, thereby finding a way to connect heaven and earth within their consciousness and experience. In this sense, the dance with the Beloved is just the fruit of a synergy that has already taken place within their own consciousness.

My tree models this more majestically than any other being I have encountered. Its reach into the sky is magical, poetic, childlike in its pure joy, but that is possible only because it is equally connected with the ground. When you look at my tree and I ask you "Which is it more: horizontal or vertical? Is it more about the male energy ascending to heaven, or about the female energy staying connected to the earth?" you will look and say "It is both at the same time."

My tree models a new kind of Tantra. It tells us to rest deeply in who we are, to trust our intuition, and to allow ourselves to grow into each other in whatever way feels good to us in the moment. It tells us to be spontaneous, but not in a rush. When we trust in our own inner rhythms, patience and spontaneity go hand in hand. The spinning clay and the hands of the potter become one.

My tree is a living meditation on centering. It is movement and stillness interpenetrating. It has a depth of center and a freedom of movement at the periphery that only a whirling dervish could understand. If Rumi had met my tree, he would have found an even greater spiritual Master than Shams of Tabriz.

Garcia Lorca understood something about the power of trees. His olive tree becomes a woman or is it the other way around? He writes:

La niña del bello rostro
*sigue cogiendo aceituna,*
*con el brazo gris del viento*
*ceñido por la cintura.*
*Arbolé, arbolé.*
*Seco y verdé.*

The girl with the pretty face
keeps on picking olives
with the grey arm of the wind
wrapped around her waist.
Tree, tree
dry and green.

Many suitors come by trying to persuade the girl to go off with them, but the girl declines. She must continue to rest in herself. Her dance is not an outward one but an inward one. She is whole inside herself. As the girl, Lorca has her picking olives. But, as the tree, she is growing them too. She is self contained and self nurtured. She brings love to herself and so she has love to offer others.

Lovers may come and pick her fruits but they cannot take her with them. She cannot be taken away from herself. She will not be uprooted.

She is happy to share her fruits because she knows there is an abundant supply. But uproot the tree and the fruit will die.

So many will come and go, but she will remain who she is and where she is. One day a suitor will come and put roots down next to her. He will grow at her side. Their branches and fruits will intermingle. You will not be able to tell where one ends and the other begins.

My tree is already in this state of bliss. He has no apparent lover, yet all who come into his presence love him and celebrate his beauty. People who have met him can never forget him. They bring their friends and family members to sit under his canopy. All who come do so with reverence and respect. Like me, they know that they are in the presence of a Master.

# The Meeting of Lover & Beloved

Lover and Beloved, male and female, sky and ground must be found inside the Self. The outer journey for love inevitably comes to an end and one realizes that if the Beloved does not live in the heart, S/he cannot be found in the world.

Who then is the soul mate? The soul mate is the one who has awakened to this truth and is able to recognize you as a reflection of herself.

Your soul mate knows who you are and who she is. She has only to look into your eyes and she knows. When you are together, words are not necessary. There is nothing to say or to do.

Even the most casual touch from her hand sends electricity through your body. When you look into her eyes, you fall into the river and cannot climb out. You must stay there until the river is finished with you.

Neither you nor she knows when that will be. You know only that when the invitation comes you must accept it.

Try as you might, you cannot be with the soul mate in this world. For as soon as you come together, the world disappears and there is just the two of you.

When she looks at you, you know that her eyes are not just eyes, but a vast ocean. Just one glance from her and you are marooned on some island in the middle of that ocean.

If you have anything that you need to do in this world, do not look into those eyes. Turn away while you have the choice. For once you look, your life as it used to be will be over.

If you have lived in the Silence of the Heart, even for a few fleeting moments, then you know this place. It is a place within you that is both peaceful and ecstatic, a place where movement and stillness become one.

In the presence of the Beloved, there is only Self. There is no other. Thus, when you rest in your heart, the Beloved is with you. You can never truly be apart from her, or she from you, as long as you remain in your heart and she remains in hers.

Sometimes we have trouble understanding this. We think that the Beloved is a person, who is separate from us and comes and goes. But the Beloved is not apart *from* us, nor even a part *of* us. The Beloved can never be reduced to a part, but always reflects the whole.

You see, the Lover does not need the Beloved. He already has her. If there is any perception of need, the Beloved cannot appear. The Beloved can be present only when the Lover knows that he is whole inside himself.

Of course, the Beloved may appear in the guise of one person or another. But the Beloved is not a person. The Beloved is a realization within consciousness made manifest.

You see the concept of the soul mate is badly misunderstood. It is imagined that the soul mate brings to the Lover some kind of love that is missing from his life. But no, this is not possible.

The soul mate can reflect only the love that is there. S/he cannot bring anything that is not there. If s/he could, s/he would be just another personification of co-dependent love.

Co-dependent love requires persons. Transcendent love goes beyond persons.

Yes, anyone can be the Beloved, but the Beloved is not just anyone. The Beloved is the Lover who has awakened to love within herself. Because she has learned to bring love to herself, she can bring love to you.

Sacred marriage is an internal event. It describes our relationship, not to some other, but to ourselves. Once this marriage happens within, love unfolds ecstatically in each moment.

At any moment, the Beloved may appear in form. At any moment the Lover may awaken to the truth within himself. These may appear to be two separate things, but they are really one and the same.

When we rest in the Silence of the Heart, the lion lies with the lamb. Lover and Beloved are entwined in one unbroken embrace.

Many people want to know how to do this, but it cannot be told. If you need to know how, you cannot do it. And if you do it you do not need to know how.

Life is spontaneous and unrehearsed. When we are ready to jump into the river, we open the door and it rises to meet us.

Those who cross the threshold must remain silent when asked about the origin or destination of love, for each must take the journey for himself when he is ready. No one can prepare him for the moment when he is asked to let go.

Until then, all lovers would be wise to remember one simple and abiding truth: there is nothing lacking within you, nothing for which you must search outside yourself. Everything that you need has been given to you. You have only to claim it.

The door opens when you turn the handle and pull it toward you. It is that simple. When you are ready, you will cross the threshold.

Until then, all this is a mystery and must remain so. If we would understand the division into bodies, we must realize the one presence within our hearts. Then we will understand that bodies are not necessary.

Then we will be free. Then we will inhabit the mystery fully, coming and going as we please.

*Namaste*

Paul Ferrini is the author of over 40 books on love, healing and forgiveness. His unique blend of spirituality and psychology goes beyond self-help and recovery into the heart of healing. His conferences, retreats, and *Affinity Group Process* have helped thousands of people deepen their practice of forgiveness and open their hearts to the divine presence in themselves and others.

For more information on Paul's work, visit the website at *www.paulferrini.com*. The website has many excerpts from Paul Ferrini's books, as well as information on his workshops and retreats. Be sure to request Paul's free email newsletter, as well as a free catalog of his books and audio products. You can also email: info@**heartwayspress.com** or write to **Heartways Press, 9 Phillips Steet, Greenfield, MA 01301.**

# New Audio Releases

## Being an Instrument of Love in Times of Planetary Crisis
*Two Talks on Individual and Collective Healing*

2 CDs   $24.95   ISBN 978-1-879159-79-2

## The Radiant Light Within
*Readings by Paul Ferrini from the Hidden Jewel &*
*Dancing with the Beloved*
1 CD   $16.95   ISBN 978-1-879159-74-7

## Real Happiness
Awakening To Our True Self
*An Introductory Talk by Paul Ferrini*
1 CD   $16.95   ISBN 978-1-879159-75-4

## Roadmap to Real Happiness
*Living the Life of Joy and Purpose*
*You Were Meant to Live*   Part 1
4 CDs   $48.00   ISBN 978-1-879159-72-3

Part 2   3 CDs   $36.00
ISBN 978-1-879159-73-0

## Creating a Life of Fulfillment
*Insights on Work, Relationship and Life Purpose*
2 CDs   $24.95
ISBN 978-1-879159-76-1

# Paul Ferrini's Course in Spiritual Mastery

## Part One: The Laws of Love
A Guide to Living in Harmony
with Universal Spiritual Truth
144 pages  $12.95
ISBN # 1-879159-60-0

## Part Two: The Power of Love
10 Spiritual Practices that Can Transform Your Life
168 pages   $12.95
ISBN # 1-879159-61-9

## Part Three: The Presence of Love
God's Answer to Humanity's Call for Help
160 pages   $12.95
ISBN # 1-879159-62-7

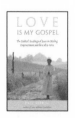

## Part Four: Love is My Gospel
The Radical Teachings of Jesus on Healing,
Empowerment and the Call to Serve
128 pages   $12.95
ISBN # 1-879159-67-8

## Part Five: Real Happiness

A Roadmap for Healing Our Pain and Awakening
the Joy That Is Our Birthright
160 pages   $12.95
ISBN # 978-1-879159-68-6

## Part Six: Embracing Our True Self

A New Paradigm Approach to Healing Our Wounds,
Finding Our Gifts, and Fulfilling Our Spiritual
Purpose
192 pages   $13.95
ISBN # 978-1-879159-69-3

## Part Seven: Real Happiness—
## The Workbook

Creating Your Personal Roadmap
to a Joyful and Empowered Life
96 pages   $14.95
ISBN # 978-1-879159-71-6

## *Paul's In-depth Presentation of the Laws of Love on 9 CDs*

## THE LAWS OF LOVE

Part One (5 CDs) ISBN # 1-879159-58-9   $49.00
Part Two (4 CDs) ISBN # 1-879159-59-7   $39.00

# Paul Ferrini's Real Happiness Workshop

By Real Happiness we mean the ability to be true to ourselves, kind to others, and able to weather the ups and downs of life with acceptance and compassion.

This powerful workshop is designed to help us learn to love and accept ourselves radically and profoundly. Participants will learn to:

• Accept, nurture and bring love to themselves.

• Be true to themselves and live honestly and authentically.

• Make and accept responsibility for their own decisions.

• Discover their talents/gifts and find their passion/purpose.

• Cultivate an open heart and an open mind.

• Forgive and learn from their mistakes.

• Be patient with the process of healing and transformation.

• Cultivate a positive attitude toward life and see obstacles as challenges.

• Develop the capacity to hear their inner guidance and surrender to their spiritual purpose.

A genuinely happy person lives in *Right Relationship* to self and others and engages in *Right Livelihood*, expressing his or her gifts and bringing joy to self and others. These are therefore the goals of this work. For more information about how you can bring this workshop to your community call us at 1-888-HARTWAY.

# Audio Workshops on CD

## Seeds of Transformation:
Set includes: Healing Without Fixing, The Wound and the Gift, Opening to the Divine Love Energy, The Laws of Love, The Path to Mastery.
5 CDs    ISBN 1-879159-63-5    $48.00

## Two Talks on Spiritual Mastery by Paul Ferrini
We are the Bringers of Love   CD 1
Surrendering to What Is   CD 2
2 CDs    ISBN 1-879159-65-1    $24.00

## Love is That Certainty
ISBN 1-879159-52-X    $16.95

## Atonement:
The Awakening of Planet Earth and its Inhabitants
ISBN 1-879159-53-8    $16.95

## From Darkness to Light:
The Soul's Journey of Redemption
ISBN 1-879159-54-6    $16.95

# Relationship Books

## Dancing with the Beloved:
Opening our Hearts to the Lessons of Love
ISBN 1-879159-47-3
160 pages paperback   $12.95

## Living in the Heart:
The Affinity Process and the Path of Unconditional Love and Acceptance
128 pages   paperback   ISBN 1-879159-36-8
$10.95

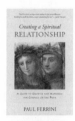

## Creating a Spiritual Relationship
128 pages   paperback
ISBN 1-879159-39-2   $10.95

## The Twelve Steps of Forgiveness
120 pages   paperback   ISBN 1-879159-10-4
$10.95

## The Ecstatic Moment:
A Practical Manual for Opening Your Heart and Staying in It
128 pages   paperback   ISBN 1-879159-18-X
$10.95

# Christ Mind Books and Audio

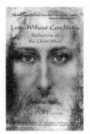

Part 1        Part 2        Part 3        Part 4

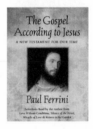

## Christ Mind Books

Love Without Conditions  ISBN 1-879159-15-5   $12.95

The Silence of the Heart  ISBN 1-879159-16-3   $14.95

Miracle of Love   ISBN 1-879159-23-6    $12.95

Return to the Garden   ISBN 1-879159-35-x    $12.95

The Living Christ  ISBN 1-879159-49-X  paperback $14.95

I am the Door  hardcover  ISBN 1-879159-41-4  $21.95

The Way of Peace  hardcover  ISBN 1-879159-42-2  $19.95

## Christ Mind Audio Read by the Author

Love Without Conditions
3 CDs ISBN 978-1-879159-64-8  $36.00

The Gospel According to Jesus Selected Readings from the
Christ Mind Teachings 2CDs  ISBN 978-1-879159-78-5  $24.95

# Wisdom Books and Audio

## Everyday Wisdom
A Spiritual Book of Days
224 pages paperback   $13.95
ISBN 1-879159-51-1

## Wisdom Cards:
Spiritual Guidance for Every Day of our Lives
ISBN 1-879159-50-3   $10.95
*Each full color card features a beautiful
painting evoking an archetypal theme*

## Forbidden Fruit:
Unraveling the Mysteries of Sin, Guilt
and Atonement
ISBN 1-879159-48-1
160 pages paperback   $12.95

## Enlightenment for Everyone
with an Introduction by Iyanla Vanzant
ISBN 1-879159-45-7
160 pages hardcover   $16.00

## The Great Way of All Beings:
Renderings of Lao Tzu
ISBN 1-879159-46-5
320 pages hardcover   $23.00

Grace Unfolding:
The Art of Living A Surrendered Life
96 pages   paperback   ISBN 1-879159-37-6   $9.95

Illuminations on the Road to Nowhere
160 pages   paperback
ISBN 1-879159-44-9   $12.95

## Audio Books

The Economy of Love  Readings from *Silence of the Heart,
The Ecstatic Moment, Grace Unfolding* and other books.
ISBN 1-879159-56-2   $16.95

Relationship as a Spiritual Path Readings from *Creating a
Spiritual Relationship, Dancing with the Beloved, Miracle of Love* and
other books.  ISBN 1-879159-55-4   $16.95

The Hands of God Readings from *Illuminations, Enlightenment
for Everyone, Forbidden Fruit, The Great Way of All Beings* and other
books.  ISBN 1-879159-57-0   $16.95

Heart and Soul Poems of Love and Awakening read by the Author.
ISBN 978-1-879159-77-8   1 CD   $16.95

# Heartways Press Order Form

Name _____

Address _____

City _____ State _____ Zip _____

Phone/Fax _____ Email* _____

*Please include your email to receive Paul's newsletter and weekly wisdom message.*

| Title ordered | quantity | price |
|---|---|---|
|  |  |  |
|  |  |  |
|  |  |  |
|  |  |  |
|  |  |  |
|  |  |  |
|  |  |  |
|  |  |  |

TOTAL _____

**Priority Shipping: one book $5.95**                    _____

**Additional books, please add $1 per book**             _____

TOTAL _____

For shipping outside the USA, or if you require rush shipping, please contact us for shipping costs

Send Order To: Heartways Press  9 Phillips Street,
Greenfield, MA 01301    413-774-9474
Toll free: 1-888-HARTWAY (Orders only)
www.PaulFerrini.com      email: info@heartwayspress.com

Please allow 1–2 weeks for delivery. Payment must be made by check or credit card (MC/VISA/AmEx) before books are shipped. Please make out your check or money order (U.S. funds only) to Heartways Press.